a.Ross

D1494252

SELECTED POEMS OF
GEORGE HERBERT

THE POETRY BOOKSHELF

General Editor: James Reeves

Robert Graves: *English and Scottish Ballads*
James Reeves: *Chaucer: Lyric and Allegory*
Tom Scott: *Late Medieval Scots Poetry*
William Tydeman: *English Poetry 1400–1580*
Martin Seymour-Smith: *Shakespeare's Sonnets*
Martin Seymour-Smith: *Longer Elizabethan Poems*
James Reeves: *John Donne*
Maurice Hussey: *Jonson and the Cavaliers*
Jack Dalglish: *Eight Metaphysical Poets*
James Reeves and Martin Seymour-Smith: *Andrew Marvell*
Dennis Burden: *Shorter Poems of John Milton*
V. de S. Pinto: *Poetry of the Restoration*
Roger Sharrock: *John Dryden*
James Reeves: *Jonathan Swift*
John Heath-Stubbs: *Alexander Pope*
Francis Venables: *The Early Augustans*
Donald Davie: *The Late Augustans*
F. W. Bateson: *William Blake*
G. S. Fraser: *Robert Burns*
Roger Sharrock: *William Wordsworth*
James Reeves: *S. T. Coleridge*
Robin Skelton: *Lord Byron*
John Holloway: *P. B. Shelley*
James Reeves: *John Clare*
Robert Gittings: *Poems and Letters of John Keats*
Edmund Blunden: *Alfred Lord Tennyson*
James Reeves: *Robert Browning*
Denys Thompson: *Poems and Prose of Matthew Arnold*
James Reeves: *Emily Dickinson*
James Reeves: *G. M. Hopkins*
David Wright: *Seven Victorian Poets*
James Reeves: *The Modern Poets' World*
James Reeves: *D. H. Lawrence*

SELECTED POEMS OF
GEORGE HERBERT

Edited with an Introduction
Commentary and Notes

by

GARETH REEVES

HEINEMANN
LONDON

Heinemann Educational Books Ltd

LONDON   EDINBURGH   MELBOURNE
SINGAPORE   JOHANNESBURG
IBADAN   HONG KONG
TORONTO   AUCKLAND
NAIROBI   NEW DELHI

ISBN 0 435 15060 x (cased edition)
ISBN 0 435 15061 8 (paperback)

GEORGE HERBERT 1593–1633

INTRODUCTION, COMMENTARY AND NOTES
© GARETH REEVES 1971

FIRST PUBLISHED 1971

Published by
Heinemann Educational Books Ltd
48 Charles Street, London W1X 8AH
Printed in Great Britain by Morrison & Gibb Ltd
London and Edinburgh

CONTENTS

FOREWORD

In this selection the text of the poems from *The Temple* is essentially
that of the first edition of 1633. Such emendations as I have made,
from the Williams MS. (referred to in the notes as W.) and from the
Bodleian MS. (B.), are recorded in the notes. The text of the two
sonnets from Walton's *Lives* is that of the 1670 edition. The text
of the extracts from *A Priest to the Temple or, The Country Parson*
is that of the 1671 (second) edition. In the notes reference is made
to the definitive edition, *The Works of George Herbert*, edited by
F. E. Hutchinson, Oxford (1941) (referred to as 'Hutchinson'); and
to *The English Works of George Herbert*, edited by G. H. Palmer,
Hodder and Stoughton, 3 volumes (1905) ('Palmer'). Throughout
I have followed the practice of B. in setting out the sonnets solid,
not as in 1633 with line-breaks between the quatrains. I have
adopted Hutchinson's numbering of those poems which bear the
same title.

INTRODUCTION

I

GEORGE HERBERT, religious poet and, for the last three years of his life, parson of a small country parish, was descended from an aristocratic family, which for over two hundred years had been one of the most distinguished in England and Wales. The fifth son of Richard and Magdalen Herbert, he was born in Montgomery on 3 April 1593. His father died when George was three years old, and to Magdalen was left the care of seven sons and three daughters; to the task of their education and guidance she devoted herself whole-heartedly.

The daughter and heiress of Sir Richard Newport, a wealthy landowner in Shropshire, she was highly intelligent, witty and charming, a woman of literary tastes, and a dedicated Christian. She knew John Donne well for over twenty years, and the best memorial to their friendship is the *Sermon of Commemoration* that he preached at her death in 1627. Here he made particular mention of her religion:

> For, as the *rule* of all her *civill Actions*, was *Religion*, so, the *rule* of her *Religion*, was the *Scripture*; And, her *rule*, for her particular understanding of the *Scripture*, was the *Church*. Shee never diverted towards the *Papist*, in undervaluing the *Scripture*; nor towards the *Separatist*, in undervaluing the *Church*.

In an age of bitter religious conflict and passionate theology her son George was never to diverge from this moderate position of the devout Anglican.

Like his ancestors, most of George's brothers actively served the Crown. Richard and William died as officers fighting in the Low Countries; Henry was knighted and became Master of the Revels;

Thomas became a captain in the navy; only Charles, who died a fellow at New College, Oxford, seems to have had the same inclinations as his brother George. The most striking comparison, however, is between George and the eldest brother, Edward, Lord Herbert of Cherbury, who achieved the greater contemporary fame. He was not only a poet, the author of at least three very fine poems (*Tears, flow no more: Elegy over a Tomb*; and *An Ode upon a Question moved, Whether Love should continue for ever?*), but also courtier, diplomat, and philosopher, propounding heretical views on religious matters. Moving in literary and court circles with equal ease, he was an outstanding example of a gentleman of the times. He seems to have combined the vitality of the Herberts with the literary tastes of his mother; George, on the other hand, seems to have had more of the mother's characteristics. Of a frailer constitution than Edward, his nature was more contemplative, and his vitality was constantly drained by moods of depression.

Yet there is evidence to indicate that George was initially as ambitious as Edward, and that he had a full complement of the characteristic Herbert traits. At the age of twelve he was sent to Westminster School, where he studied Greek and Latin; it was here also that he gained considerable knowledge of music and learnt to play the lute—facts which should be remembered when considering the mastery of his lyric verse and the numerous references to music which it contains. Of Herbert's university days Izaak Walton, in his *Life of Mr. George Herbert*, wrote:

> all, or the greatest diversion from his Study, was the practice of Musick, in which he became a great Master; and of which, he would say, 'That it did relieve his drooping spirits, compose his distracted thoughts, and raised his weary soul so far above Earth, that it gave him an earnest of the joys of Heaven, before he possest them.'

From Westminster Herbert gained a scholarship to Trinity College, Cambridge, where he quickly distinguished himself, becoming a fellow and a college lecturer. Lack of funds and ill-health, however, were two constant sources of worry to him at university. He explained his situation in a letter of 1618 to Sir John Danvers, his youthful step-father whom Magdalen had married in middle age and who seems to have treated Herbert generously:

> You know I was sick last Vacation, neither am I yet recovered, so that I am fain ever and anon, to buy somewhat tending towards my health; for infirmities are both painful and costly. Now this *Lent* I am forbid utterly to eat any Fish, so that I am fain to dyet in my Chamber at mine own cost; for in our publick Halls, you know, is nothing but Fish and Whit-meats: Out of *Lent* also, twice a Week, on *Fridayes* and *Saturdayes*, I must do so, which yet sometimes I fast. Sometimes also I ride to *Newmarket*, and there lie a day or two for fresh Air; all which tend to avoiding of costlier matters, if I should fall absolutely sick: I protest and vow, I even study Thrift, and yet I am scarce able with much ado to make one half years allowance, shake hands with the other: And yet if a Book of four or five Shillings come in my way, I buy it, though I fast for it; yea, sometimes of Ten Shillings: But, alas Sir, what is that to those infinite Volumes of Divinity, which yet every day swell, and grow bigger.

At Cambridge Herbert composed many of the first versions of poems later to appear in *The Temple*, the volume of poetry published shortly after his death. In his first year at Trinity he sent his mother two sonnets, remarkable performances for a seventeen-year-old, advocating religious rather than secular love as the subject for poetry (see p. 108); with them he sent this letter:

> But I fear the heat of my late *Ague* hath dried up those springs, by which Scholars say, the Muses use to take up their habitations. However, I need not their help, to reprove the vanity of those many Love-poems, that are daily writ and consecrated to *Venus*; nor to bewail that so few are writ, that look towards *God* and *Heaven*. For my own part, my meaning (*dear Mother*) is in these Sonnets, to declare my resolution to be, that my poor Abilities in *Poetry* shall be all, and ever consecrated to Gods glory; and I beg you to receive this as one testimony.

Though Herbert was to vacillate over his decision to take holy orders, he was never to go back on this dedication of his poetry to God.

Though his mother, it seems, had early prepared Herbert for the vocation of holy orders, he periodically held back from such a step. Undoubtedly the reasons were manifold, for Herbert's was a highly complex nature, pulled by many opposing forces. It is certain, however, that his ambitious aspirations had a lot to do with his hesitancy. At this time Herbert lived not without vanity and ostentation; even Walton, who is at pains to emphasize his saintliness, writes:

> if during this time he exprest any Error, it was, that he kept himself too much retir'd, and at too great a distance with all his inferiours: and his cloaths seem'd to prove, that he put too great a value on his parts and Parentage.

After gaining his first university office of Reader in Rhetoric, Herbert strongly desired to become Public Orator to the University; it was a post which would improve his finances, and which was at the same time of considerable prestige. In September 1619 he wrote to Sir John Danvers:

> The Orators place (that you may understand what it is) is the finest place in the University, though not the gainfullest; yet that will be about 30 *l. per an.* but the commodiousness is beyond the Revenue; for the Orator writes all the University Letters, makes all the Orations, be it to King, Prince, or whatever comes to the University; to requite these pains, he takes place next the Doctors, is at all their Assemblies and Meetings, and sits above the Proctors, is Regent or Non-regent at his pleasure, and such like Gaynesses, which will please a young man well.

There is little doubt that Herbert regarded the post as a stepping-stone to some high civil employment; Sir Francis Nethersole, who was then Public Orator, and his predecessor Sir Robert Naunton, both became Secretaries of State. When Sir Francis Nethersole objected that perhaps the post was not right for Herbert, Herbert explained himself thus, in a letter to Sir John Danvers of October 1619:

> I understand by Sir *Francis Nethersols* Letter, that he fears I have not fully resolved of the matter, since this place being civil may divert me

4

too much from Divinity, at which, not without cause, he thinks, I aim; but, I have wrote him back, that this dignity, hath no such earthiness in it, but it may very well be joined with Heaven; or if it had to others, yet to me it should not, for ought I yet knew.

No doubt the letter is in part sincere; to Herbert at this time there was no discrepancy in first seeking to fulfil his secular ambitions, and then aiming at the priesthood. Indeed, it is probable that he considered it highly suitable for a religious man to put his skills in civil affairs to the service of the Christian state; such was the case of his friend Bishop Lancelot Andrewes, himself a member of the Privy Council. In any event, Herbert rallied all the influential support possible to secure the post, and in 1620 he succeeded.

Through the Oratorship he came into contact with the court of James I, and even with the King himself. According to Walton, by this time:

He had acquir'd great Learning, and was blest with a high fancy, a civil and sharp wit, and with a natural elegance, both in his behaviour, his tongue, and his pen.

He evidently made use of this learning, wit, and charm to please James I. The only occasion on which he ventured into religious controversy was when he wrote a violent attack against the Puritan zealot, Andrew Melville, who had strongly denounced Anglican ritual; no doubt the attack was sincere, but Herbert's main concern was probably to win the approval of the King. In his first year of office he composed a letter of thanks for James I on behalf of the University, together with three complimentary verses in Latin.

This Letter [wrote Walton] was writ in such excellent Latin, was so full of Conceits, and all the expressions so suted to the *genius* of the King, that he inquired the Orators name, and then ask'd *William* Earl of *Pembroke*, if he knew him? whose answer was, 'That he knew him very well; and that he was his Kinsman, but he lov'd him more for his learning and vertue, than for that he was of his name and family.' At which answer, the King smil'd, and asked the Earl leave, 'that he might love him too; for he took him to be the Jewel of that University.'

At this time Herbert's friendship with Bishop Andrewes was growing, and he assiduously cultivated a friendship with the Lord Chancellor, Francis Bacon, whom Herbert greatly admired despite the very different outlooks of the two men. Bacon dedicated to him his *Translation of Certaine Psalmes* and had him translate parts of *The Advancement of Learning*. For his last three years as Orator Herbert was seldom at Cambridge, but, as Walton explains:

> the love of a Court-conversation mixt with a laudible ambition to be something more than he then was, drew him often from *Cambridge* to attend the *King* wheresoever the Court was.

For seven years Herbert held the post of Orator, yet in all that time he obtained no form of employment from the Court. Walton put this down to the deaths in rapid succession of his friends and patrons; between 1624 and 1626 Bacon, Andrewes, and other influential acquaintances all died. Walton continues:

> King *James* died also, and with them, all Mr. *Herbert's* Court-hopes: So that he presently betook himself to a Retreat from *London*, to a Friend in *Kent*, where he liv'd very privately, and was such a lover of solitariness, as was judg'd to impair his health, more then his Study had done. In this time of Retirement, he had many Conflicts with himself, Whether he should return to the painted pleasures of a Court-life, or betake himself to a study of Divinity, and enter into Sacred Orders? (to which his dear Mother had often persuaded him.) These were such Conflicts, as they only can know, that have endur'd them; for ambitious Desires, and the outward Glory of this World, are not easily laid aside; but, at last, God inclin'd him to put on a resolution to serve at his Altar.

The chain of events which affected Herbert's attitude, however, seems to have been more complex than Walton implies. Earlier, as has been remarked, Herbert saw no disparity between serving God and serving the Crown. It was only when he began to doubt this conviction that the choice between civil and 'divine' employment had to be faced; and it was events in 1624 and 1625 that raised these doubts. The deaths of his friends and patrons may have helped to precipitate his decision, but they can have had little to do with his change in attitude.

In 1624 Herbert was elected M.P. for Montgomery, and attended James I's last Parliament, a session which must have made high office at Court seem undesirable. In the important area of foreign policy the different factions wanted war—but different wars: King James wanted above all to recover the Palatinate, but Prince Charles and his supporter Buckingham were determined to have war with Spain. To Herbert, as a peace-loving man, these alternatives must have seemed equally uncongenial. He had made his attitude clear the previous year, when Charles, after an unsuccessful attempt to gain the hand of the Spanish Infanta, returned to England bent on war with Spain. It was Herbert's job to speak at the Cambridge celebration on the occasion of Charles's safe return; and in this, his most important oration, he could not refrain from commending Charles for going to Spain in search of peace. It was not a speech to please the Prince and future King. Herbert can hardly have looked forward to Charles's first Parliament, in 1625, particularly as Edward Herbert had been recalled from France in disgrace. After this session, which proved to be as divisive as the previous, with Parliament adamantly opposed to Charles and Buckingham, any Court hopes remaining with Herbert must have disappeared entirely. In such circumstances Church office and State employment would have seemed no longer compatible to Herbert.

In any event, after a period of retirement, Herbert resolved to take holy orders, and in 1626 he was ordained deacon. At that time it was a decisive and unusual step for a man of his high birth, for, although it did not commit him to parochial life, it debarred him from further civil employment. No doubt he was influenced in his decision by his mother, Bishop Andrewes, and Donne, who was now Dean of St. Paul's and who was with Herbert during part of his retirement. There was also the precedent of his great friend Nicholas Ferrar, who had attended the 1624 Parliament with

Herbert, and had subsequently retired from the world to Little Gidding; it was here that he carried out a unique experiment in the creation of a domestic religious community.

For some time Herbert hung back from the further step of committing himself to parochial life. In part this was due to his worsening health. In 1626, recounts Walton, 'Mr. *Herbert* was seiz'd with a sharp *Quotidian Ague*, and thought to remove it by the change of Air'. He went to live with his brother, Sir Henry, at Woodford, Essex, for about a year, where, according to Walton, by means of 'a constant Dyet, he remov'd his Ague, but with inconveniences that were worse; for he brought upon himself a disposition to Rheums, and other weaknesses, and a supposed Consumption'. It must also have taken some time for Herbert to reconcile himself to the obscure life of parish priest; Barnabas Oley, an early biographer, wrote that he had 'heard sober men censure him as a man that did not manage his brave parts to his best advantage and preferment, but lost himself *in an humble way*; That was the phrase, I well remember it'. For someone as gifted, high-born, and proud as Herbert, with early hopes of a promising career, this must have been a particularly irritating censure. Most commentators agree it was during these years, 1626 to 1629, that he composed many of the poems of indecision and discontent. There are some poems, such as *Aaron* and *The Priesthood*, which indicate that his hesitancy was also the result of a sense of unworthiness, a feeling that he was not fit to serve God. As Walton put it, there was in him an 'apprehension of the last great Account that he was to make for the Cure of so many Souls'.

Herbert went to stay for a time with Lord Danvers, his step-father's elder brother. His health improved, and in 1629 he married Jane Danvers, the daughter of a cousin of Lord Danvers; though in detail Walton's account is probably inaccurate, it is a charming story:

this Mr. *Danvers* having known him long, and familiarly, did so much affect him, that he often and publickly declar'd a desire that Mr. *Herbert* would marry any of his Nine Daughters (for he had so many) but rather

8

his Daughter *Jane*, than any other, because *Jane was his beloved Daughter*: And he had often said the same to Mr. *Herbert* himself; and that if he could like her for a Wife, and she him for a Husband, *Jane* should have a *double blessing*: and Mr. *Danvers* had so often said the like to *Jane*, and so much commended Mr. *Herbert* to her, that *Jane* became so much a Platonick, as to fall in love with Mr. *Herbert* unseen.

In 1630 Herbert accepted the living of Bemerton, near Salisbury. Walton's description of the induction indicates how seriously Herbert regarded his new position:

When at his Induction he was shut into *Bemerton* Church, being left there alone to Toll the Bell, (as the Law requires him:) he staid so much longer than an ordinary time, before he return'd to those Friends that staid expecting him at the Church-door, that his Friend, Mr. *Woodnot*, look'd in at the Church-window, and saw him lie prostrate on the ground before the Altar: at which time and place (as he after told Mr. *Woodnot*) he set some Rules to himself, for the future manage of his life; and then and there made a vow, to labour to keep them.

During the last three years of his life Herbert was extraordinarily active. The rectory and two small churches at Bemerton were badly in need of repair; he restored all three out of his own pocket. Although he had far less means than his surviving brothers, Edward and Henry, he made a home for the three orphaned daughters of his sister, Margaret Vaughan. It is possible that he was also chaplain to the Earl of Pembroke. Of his brother's dedication to his vocation Lord Herbert of Cherbury wrote in his autobiography: 'His life was most holy and exemplary; insomuch, that about Salisbury, where he lived, beneficed for many years, he was little less than sainted.' Nicholas Ferrar, in his preface to *The Temple*, wrote: 'As God had enabled him, so he accounted him meet not onely to be called, but to be compelled to this service: Wherein his faithfull discharge was such, as may make him justly a companion to the primitive Saints, and a pattern or more for the age he lived in.' It is this aspect of Herbert's life which Walton wished to stress, and he gives a delightful tribute to it in this anecdote:

9

In another walk to *Salisbury*, he saw a poor man, with a poorer horse, that was fall'n under his Load; they were both in distress, and needed present help; which Mr. *Herbert* perceiving, put off his Canonical Coat, and help'd the poor man to unload, and after, to load his horse: The poor man blest him for it: and he blest the poor man; and was so like the *good Samaritan*, that he gave him money to refresh both himself and his horse; and told him, *That if he lov'd himself, he should be merciful to his Beast.*—Thus he left the poor man, and at his coming to his musical friends at *Salisbury*, they began to wonder that Mr. *George Herbert* which us'd to be so trim and clean, came into that company so soyl'd and discompos'd; but he told them the occasion: And when one of the company told him, *He had disparag'd himself by so dirty an employment*; his answer was, *That the thought of what he had done, would prove Musick to him at Midnight; and that the omission of it, would have upbraided and made discord in his Conscience, whensoever he should pass by that place; for, if I be bound to pray for all that be in distress, I am sure that I am bound so far as it is in my power to practice what I pray for. And though I do not wish for the like occasion every day, yet let me tell you, I would not willingly pass one day of my life without comforting a sad soul, or shewing mercy; and I praise God for this occasion:* And now let's tune our Instruments.

The years at Bemerton were also the period of Herbert's greatest literary activity. He translated *A Treatise of Temperance and Sobrietie*, about how to preserve life and health into old age, written at the age of 83 by a sixteenth-century Venetian, Luigi Cornaro. He wrote *A Priest to the Temple or, The Country Parson, His Character and Rule of Holy Life*, a practical manual on the parish priest's duties and way of life, and our surest indication of Herbert's practice as a country parson; extracts appear in this selection, after the poems. Most important of all, at Bemerton Herbert revised many of his earlier poems and wrote more than half the poems in *The Temple*. Those inward conflicts that characterize the poems written during the period of indecision are less evident in the Bemerton poems. In the later group there are, however, occasional indications of despondency, and anxiety that his bad health kept him from his priestly duties. Increasing illness made him less and less able to perform these

duties, and after only three years of ministry he died on 1 March
1633.

How Herbert regarded his poetry is indicated by the words he
spoke, at the approach of death, on entrusting his book of poems
to his dearest friend, Nicholas Ferrar. Walton wrote:

> he did with so sweet a humility as seem'd to exalt him, bow down to
> Mr. *Duncon*, and with a thoughtful and contented look, say to him,—
> *Sir, I pray deliver this little Book to my dear brother* Farrer, *and tell him, he
> shall find in it a picture of the many spiritual Conflicts that have past betwixt
> God and my Soul, before I could subject mine to the will of* Jesus my Master:
> *in whose service I have now found perfect freedom; desire him to read it: and
> then, if he can think it may turn to the advantage of any dejected poor Soul,
> let it be made publick: if not, let him burn it: for* I and it, are less than the
> least of God's mercies.

Though some early Latin poems by Herbert had been published
during his lifetime, none of his English poems had appeared in
print. They must, however, have been circulated in manuscript,
since he enjoyed some reputation as a poet during his lifetime;
Bacon, in the dedication to Herbert of his *Translation of Certaine
Psalmes*, wrote:

> it being my manner for Dedications, to choose those that I hold most
> fit for the Argument, I thought, that in respect of Divinitie, and Poesie,
> met (whereof the one is the Matter, the other the Stile of this little
> Writing) I could not make better choice.

Ferrar arranged for the publication of *The Temple* within a year of
Herbert's death; it was an immediate success, and within three years
four editions appeared. Its popularity continued to the end of the
century, and it had considerable influence on subsequent poets.
Richard Crashaw entitled his first volume of English sacred verse
Steps to the Temple (1646). But Henry Vaughan's debt to Herbert
was very much greater than Crashaw's; Vaughan followed closely
Herbert's subjects and titles, and his poetry is packed with quotations
and echoes from *The Temple*. Throughout the eighteenth century

Herbert's poetic reputation steadily declined. His memory was kept alive by only a few people, the most notable being John Wesley; he popularized many poems from *The Temple* by including them (often with the metrical patterns considerably altered) in collections of hymns and sacred poems, though they were appreciated more for their piety than for their poetry. William Cowper was one of the few men of letters in the eighteenth century to mention Herbert's poems favourably, but even he reflects the general opinion of the age; in his *Memoirs* he wrote, 'gothic and uncouth as they were, I yet found in them a strain of piety which I could not but admire'. The restoration of Herbert's reputation was begun by Coleridge, who, in a letter of 1818 to William Collins, wrote:

> I find more substantial comfort now in pious George Herbert's 'Temple' which I used to read to amuse myself with his quaintness—in short, only to laugh at—than in all the poetry since the poems of Milton. If you have not read Herbert, I can recommend the book to you confidently. The poem entitled 'The Flower' is especially affecting; and, to me, such a phrase as 'and relish versing' expresses a sincerity, a reality, which I would unwillingly exchange for the more dignified 'and once more love the Muse' &c. And so, with many other of Herbert's homely phrases.

II

Herbert is one of a number of poets who have been labelled 'metaphysical'. The epithet derives from a comment of Dryden's of 1693, and was adapted, long after the poets concerned were dead, by Dr. Johnson in his *Life of Cowley*: 'about the beginning of the seventeenth century appeared a race of writers that may be termed the metaphysical poets'. Johnson was being disparaging, and did not consider that these poets were 'metaphysical' in the true sense. The term 'metaphysical poets', however, has remained as a convenient label for those poets who in the seventeenth century wrote under the influence of John Donne (1572–1631); they include Herbert, Thomas Carew (1594/5–1640), Richard Crashaw (1612–49),

Abraham Cowley (1618–67), Henry Vaughan (1621–95), and Andrew Marvell (1621–78). In the period which these poets span there are of course many variations in the practice of writing metaphysical poetry, and any generalizations will inevitably present a partial view.

Nevertheless, it is possible to define certain characteristics which are common to the metaphysical poets, and to point to qualities in Donne's writing which recur, in one form or another, in the poetry of his successors. Perhaps the most striking similarity between Donne and the other metaphysicals is the way in which the poem develops by a process of logical argument; the reader is made to follow a progression of thought in which an understanding of each step is necessary for an understanding of the whole; we see this quality very clearly in Herbert's *Mortification*, and in the beautifully worked-out argument of *Man*. Thus the intellect plays a great part in metaphysical poetry; the mental dexterity, sharp wit, and delight in the free play of the intellect which characterize Donne's poetry are very apparent in Herbert's; examine for instance *The Quip*, or the paradox at the close of *Affliction (I)*. There is a considerable amount of verbal play in Herbert, the most drawn-out example being *Clasping of Hands*; the style is very reminiscent of Donne:

> Or if then thou gav'st mee all
> All was but All, which thou hadst then.
> (*Loves Infiniteness* ll.12–13)

A notable characteristic of metaphysical poetry is its dramatic quality; it is important to remember that the earlier of these poets developed their manner in the great age of English drama, the age of Shakespeare. In both Donne and Herbert there is a subtle mastery of speech rhythms, and a dexterity in playing off the natural voice rhythm against a formal metrical pattern; both poets (though Donne to a greater extent) use the forceful opening—in Donne for instance, 'Busie old foole, unruly Sunne' (*The Sunne Rising*), 'For Godsake hold your tongue, and let me love' (*The Canonization*), 'Batter my heart, three person'd God' (*Holy Sonnets* XIV); and in Herbert,

'Full of rebellion, I would die' (*Nature*), 'Peace mutt'ring thoughts, and do not grudge to keep' (*Content*), and 'Broken in pieces all asunder' (*Affliction* (*IV*). A third dramatic characteristic in both poets is dialogue; even when Donne is not addressing another person or God he usually carries on a dialogue with himself; the majority of Herbert's poems are colloquies with God.

Herbert's debt to Donne should not be overstressed; later in the Introduction, in the more detailed discussion of the poetry, I shall point to some differences, especially in their use of imagery and metaphor, and shall indicate some of the qualities which make Herbert's poetry unique. There are also other traditions apart from the metaphysical which should be recognized in a consideration of Herbert's poetry. An influential figure who affected the writing of many poets of this period was Ben Jonson (1573–1637), who established a direction complementary to that started by Donne. Jonson's poetry is characterized by terse exactitude, the blending of pointed and racy speech with graceful forms, and a genial yet cultivated manner; all these qualities are to be found in Herbert's poetry. But Herbert was influenced more particularly by a poet of an earlier generation, Sir Philip Sidney (1554–86), who was in some sense a predecessor to Jonson. His love poems, the sonnet sequence *Astrophel and Stella*, have more of the mellifluousness and studied eloquence of the Elizabethan manner; but there is also, in the best of his poems, a blending of logical subtlety and dexterity with honesty and tenderness which we see also in Herbert's poetry. Sidney was also one of the greatest Elizabethan experimenters in the lyric; it is very likely that Herbert read, and was influenced by, his metrical versions of the first forty-three psalms, where Sidney experimented in a variety of metres and verse-forms.

Herbert is the only metaphysical poet who was inspired solely by his religious faith. Donne's reputation rests mainly upon the secular love poetry he wrote in the earlier years of his life; had he never written the divine poems of later years his distinction would be little diminished. Though most highly regarded today for his devotional poetry, Crashaw composed some notable secular verse.

The only seventeenth-century poet comparable with Herbert in this respect is Henry Vaughan; but even he began by writing, mostly unremarkable, secular love poetry. Herbert's early dedication of his poetry to God is unique, and it produced some of the finest religious lyrics in the English language.

When, in his *Life of Waller*, Dr. Johnson found fault with devotional poetry, he perhaps expressed what many instinctively feel. He argued that a man who is divinely possessed is already outside and above the limitations of poetry:

> Contemplative piety, or the intercourse between God and the human soul, cannot be poetical. Man, admitted to implore the mercy of his Creator, and plead the merits of his Redeemer, is already in a higher state than poetry can confer.

But one of the most important characteristics of Herbert's poetry is the reiterated concern that this 'intercourse between God and the human soul' is so hard to acquire—'How should I praise thee, Lord!' begins *The Temper* (*I*). Throughout Herbert's poetry this concern is, as I hope to show later, part of a wider struggle to see himself in relation to God and God's created world. It is this internal conflict which gives an abiding human interest to *The Temple*, the 'little Book' which Herbert entrusted to Ferrar with those words:

> *a picture of the many spiritual Conflicts that have past betwixt God and my Soul, before I could subject mine to the will of* Jesus my Master.

Because of the abiding human interest of *The Temple* there is no necessity to *share* Herbert's Christian beliefs in order to value his poetry, any more than it is necessary to share Wordsworth's 'philosophy' of nature to appreciate *The Prelude*. However, after the initial enjoyment of a poem, appreciation is deepened by an understanding of those beliefs. This is not to say that Herbert's poetry is doctrinal; on the contrary, in the seventeenth century, an age of passionate theology, the poetry was read by high and low church Christians alike. However, time and time again the overall sense, and also subtleties in imagery and vocabulary, are clarified by a recognition of particular references. For Herbert the major sphere of reference is of course the Bible, and his contemporary readers would have been thoroughly familiar with it. I should point out here that there is a strongly traditional element in his use of the Scriptures; as the work of Rosemond Tuve has shown, many of the paradoxes and symbolic meanings derived from Scripture have their counterpart in medieval liturgy and scriptural commentaries, and can also be paralleled in medieval poetry.

Often the Biblical references in Herbert's poetry are easily recognizable; usually a basic knowledge of a particular Bible story is enough to comprehend the sense of a poem or image. There are, however, many occasions when Biblical information of a more complex nature deepens the understanding of a poem. In *The Bunch of Grapes* (p. 82), for instance, the title indicates the central Biblical image around which the poem revolves. The first stanza poses Herbert's problem—the lack of joy in his life—and ends by introducing traditional Biblical imagery of Canaan and the Red Sea. In the next stanza the poet expands on this last parallel by explaining that the wandering of the Israelites from Egypt to the Promised Land prefigures every Christian's journey between sin and heaven; in the third stanza Herbert enumerates some of the likenesses. This, however, brings him to the realization that at least the Israelites had a foretaste, in the cluster of Eschol (see note to *l*.19, p. 154), of the joy promised them; if he has their sorrows, their 'sands and serpents, tents and shrowds' (*l*.17), may he not have some proof, as they had, of joy to come? The final stanza answers Herbert's question: the bunch of grapes not only represents promise of joy, but also Christ's love for man at the Crucifixion, for the communion, for joy already attained. The grapes of Eschol, like Noah's vine (*l*.24), represent the Law of the Old Testament (see note to *l*.24, p. 154), but Christ, who was 'pressed for my sake' (*l*.28) on the Cross is the love which is the message of the New Testament. Thus Herbert's search for joy results in his realization that, through God's grace, he already possesses it. In this poem it will be seen that the image of the bunch of grapes controls the structure and development of the poem.

In contrast, there are Biblical references and overtones which are of purely local significance. Often an apparently arbitrary or strange word can be accounted for by its Biblical usage. Examine, for example, lines 5–6 of *The Thanksgiving* (p. 42):

> Shall I weep bloud? why thou hast wept such store
> That all thy body was one doore.

The overt reference of these lines is to Christ's Agony in the Garden: 'his sweat was as it were great drops of blood falling down to the ground' (Luke 22.44). By its association of tears with blood the Biblical reference already points forward to the Crucifixion. What, then, is the significance of 'doore' here? It would not, I think, be stretching the limits of association too far to refer to a use of the word in John 10.9, where Christ says, 'I am the door: by me if any man enter in, he shall be saved, and shall go in and out, and find pasture.' Because Christ sacrificed himself at the Crucifixion it is possible for man to be saved. Christ's body was the door through which the tears and blood of his suffering sprang; by means of that suffering he is our door to heaven. This may seem a round-about way of approaching Herbert's use of language. But I wish to stress here that his vocabulary is steeped in the Bible, and for the poet such a lengthy process of thought would not have been necessary. Tears, blood, the Crucifixion, the way to heaven, door, would have been for him a subconscious structure of Biblical association. Thus, for a full appreciation of Herbert's vocabulary a modern reader not well versed in the Scriptures will need to do some unravelling. In the notes at the end of this selection I have attempted to point out not only the necessary Scriptural knowledge for a basic understanding of the poems, but also some of the slighter, but nevertheless important, echoes of the Bible. Completeness in this last respect would be impossible within the limits of this selection. There is in fact much work to be done in this field; but any reader who is curious about the use of a particular word or phrase is urged to consult a Biblical concordance. Such unravelling is not of course the end of the process of appreciation; afterwards, the images and

17

vocabulary should be allowed to echo and re-echo as they did in the mind of their author.

There are other, perhaps less direct, influences of the Bible on Herbert's poetry. Many critics have noted the 'homely' and non-erudite quality of his metaphors. This is a generalization which should not be pressed too far, for, as he demonstrates in *The Pearl*, Herbert 'knows the ways of learning'. However, he certainly goes less far afield than Donne for his analogies, and there are many references to gardening, carpentry, and everyday activity; for a succession of such analogies look, for instance, at the first three stanzas of *Confession* (p. 79). Of conceits and wit I shall say more later, but the point I wish to make here is that the non-erudite quality of metaphor is undoubtedly one influence of the Bible. Herbert himself made the point in *The Country Parson* (Chapter 21):

> This is the skill, and doubtlesse the Holy Scripture intends thus much, when it condescends to the naming of a plough, a hatchet, a bushell, leaven, boyes piping and dancing; shewing that things of ordinary use are not only to serve in the way of drudgery, but to be washed, and cleansed, and serve for lights even of Heavenly Truths.

We can see too an indirect kind of influence of the Bible in a poem such as *Redemption* (p. 45), where the quasi-allegorical account of God's granting of Grace, with analogies of tenant and rich landlord, is very reminiscent of Biblical parable.

III

Herbert's great spiritual struggle was the constant effort to find and to praise God, to attain that 'intercourse between God and the human soul'. He wrote a number of poems on the subject of poetry, and from a study of some of these we shall learn more exactly what was involved in that effort.

The two sonnets *Love I* and *II*, *Jordan (I)*, *Jordan (II)* and *Dulnesse* are among the poems about poetry. *Love I* (p. 53) bewails the fact that mortal love has usurped the title of heavenly love, for man has concentrated his praise not on the Creator, but on the thing created:

> How hath man parcel'd out thy glorious name,
> And thrown it on that dust which thou hast made,
> While mortall love doth all the title gain!   (*ll.*3–5)

Mortal love, continues Herbert, has joined with 'invention'—here meaning the matter which the imagination finds for the embodiment of the poet's abstract conception (see note to *l.*6, p. 133)—leaving no room for immortal love, with the result that:

> Wit fancies beautie, beautie raiseth wit:
>   The world is theirs; they two play out the game,
>   Thou standing by.   (*ll.*9–11)

In other words, the intellect of the poet and its object, mortal beauty, are so involved in mutual advancement, that immortal love is entirely excluded. In *Love II* Herbert asks that the 'greater flame' of 'Immortall Heat' should 'Attract the lesser to it'. It is then that man's imagination will be redirected towards heavenly love:

> then shall our brain
> All her invention on thine Altar lay.   (*ll.*6–7)

As a result, the situation will no longer be one where 'Wit fancies beautie, beautie raiseth wit', but where 'Our eies shall see thee, which before saw dust'; the poet will again be able to look beyond the thing created, to the Creator (the 'dust' here is the same 'dust which thou hast made' of *Love I*). Herbert does not say, however, that in order to praise God 'wit' will have to disappear, as the last lines make clear:

> all wits shall rise,
> And praise him who did make and mend our eies.   (*ll.*13–14)

The poet is making the point that a difference exists between the wit that 'plays out the game' and a wit that makes hymns of praise.

Jordan (I) (p. 55) makes more explicit what that difference is. The first stanza juxtaposes the problem of technique with that of subject-matter:

> Is all good structure in a winding stair?
> May no lines passe, except they do their dutie
>   Not to a true, but painted chair?   (*ll.*3–5)

Cannot good verses be made in praise of heavenly love, which occupies the true throne; must we use the 'winding' structure employed by those who praise its imitator, earthly love, which occupies only a painted throne? He goes on to indicate the qualities of the 'winding stair' structure. The 'enchanted groves', 'sudden arbours' and 'purling streams' represent the paraphernalia of the pastoral love poets; while the lines

> Must all be vail'd, while he that reades, divines,
>   Catching the sense at two removes?   (*ll.*9–10)

no doubt refer to the verbal play and recondite metaphysical conceits of his contemporaries. The main point here, however, is that, to do credit to his 'true' subject, he wants neither irrelevant matter nor false manner to throttle his verse. The last stanza makes plain that he is not condemning outright the 'shepherds'—the writers of eclogue, lyric, elegy, pastoral, etc.—but merely that their way is not his: 'Shepherds are honest people; let them sing' (*l.*11). His way is to be the way of directness, of plain speaking, without, at the same time, being deficient in the art of making a 'good structure':

> Nor let them punish me with losse of ryme,
>   Who plainly say, *My God, My King.*   (*ll.*14–15)

Many critics have pointed out that *Jordan* (*I*), the poem in which Herbert defends plainness, is itself flamboyant, both in style and in range of reference. We can, it is true, regard it as a delightful play on the style he is attacking. Yet *Jordan* (*I*) is a comparatively early poem (it appears in the early Williams manuscript), and later, in *Jordan* (*II*) (p. 73) particularly, Herbert was to condemn some of his earlier practices. In *Jordan* (*II*) he accuses himself of an over-elaborate style:

> My thoughts began to burnish, sprout, and swell,
> Curling with metaphors a plain intention,
> Decking the sense, as if it were to sell.   (*ll*.4–6)

The reason for this ostentation in his past practice is given in the final stanza:

> As flames do work and winde, when they ascend,
> So did I weave my self into the sense.   (*ll*.13–14)

The fault, as Herbert sees it, was one of pride; he was more interested in demonstrating his own facility in making poetry than in the poem's 'plain intention'. The self-accusation considerably widens the boundaries of Herbert's discussion, for spiritual vanity and over-subtle style are here regarded as two aspects of the single problem of how to dedicate his poetry to God. The last lines of the poem are a restatement of Herbert's concept of directness, but now inextricably combined with the problem of integrity:

> But while I bustled, I might heare a friend
> Whisper, *How wide is all this long pretence!*
> *There is in love a sweetnesse readie penn'd:*
> *Copie out onely that, and save expense.*   (*ll*.15–18)

The humility and integrity Herbert advocates in *Jordan* (*II*) are very apparent in the poem *Dulnesse* (p. 77). Again, the comparison is between divine and secular love poetry; but the self-indulgent manner of *Love I* and *II* and *Jordan* (*I*) is replaced by a more humble and self-deprecatory tone:

> Where are my lines then? my approaches? views?
>   Where are my window-songs?
> Lovers are still pretending, & ev'n wrongs
>   Sharpen their Muse.   (*ll*.17–20)

Though the tone is different, the argument is reminiscent of *Love I* and *II*. God is 'Beautie alone to me', so that all earthly existence is a reflection of that one beauty:

21

> When all perfections as but one appeare,
> > That those thy form doth show,
> > The very dust, where thou dost tread and go,
> > > Makes beauties here. (*ll.*13–16)

Why, therefore, is he incapable of being inspired by God's 'beauties' to sing His praises, while even the secular love poets are inspired by 'wrongs'? The answer is in the sixth stanza:

> But I am lost in flesh, whose sugred lyes
> > Still mock me, and grow bold:
> Sure thou didst put a minde there, if I could
> > > Finde where it lies. (*ll.*21–4)

He cannot praise God, because his mind has been beguiled away from Him by the 'beauties'; his mind is flesh-covered, and therefore unable to perceive Him. The final stanza is a prayer that this mind may be cleared of the false deceptions created by the world, so that the poet may see God. As in *Love II* Herbert is not asking that wit should disappear from his poetry, only that it may be put to proper use:

> Lord, cleare thy gift, that with a constant wit
> > I may but look towards thee. (*ll.*25–6)

In *Love I* and *II* the argument ran thus: by laying his imaginative faculties on God's altar the poet would be able to look beyond the thing created to the Creator. Similarly in *Dulnesse*, with the aid of God's intervention the poet will no longer be deceived by the world, but will see in its beauties the Creator.

In all these poems, then, Herbert reveals a oneness of outlook in which dedication, humility, and a clear view of God's world are regarded as integral parts of the total effort to find and to praise God. In the next section of the Introduction I shall attempt to show how this oneness of outlook affected the writing of his finest poetry.

It is relevant to add at this point in the discussion an important footnote. As Rosemond Tuve points out, we should not see in any of these poems an indictment of any particular poets or schools of poetry. To be sure, Herbert is favouring divine as opposed to secular love poetry, and perhaps refers to some of the stylistic modes of his metaphysical contemporaries. But, as Miss Tuve writes of *Jordan (I)* (and it is true of all these poems), this is 'not a protest against love poetry but against its usurpation of the whole field and very title of poetry'. And the poems are not so much an indictment of other practitioners as a meditation on the nature of poetry. Indeed, Herbert borrowed to a considerable extent from Sidney, perhaps one of the 'shepherds' of *Jordan (I)*. *Jordan (II)* itself, for instance, has close echoes of Sidney's first and third sonnets in *Astrophel and Stella*, as the notes indicate (see notes, p. 148); and the famous verbal play at the end of *Affliction (I)*—'Let me not love thee, if I love thee not'—is an echo of the last line of Sidney's Sonnet 62 —'Deere, love me not, that thou may love me more'.

IV

If we place alongside poems such as *Jordan (I)* and *Church-monuments* other poems by Herbert such as *The Flower* and *Love (III)* we can appreciate the great variety of Herbert's poetic technique. It is in such poems as these last two where Herbert achieves that directness which he discusses in the poems already examined. In *The Flower* (p. 96), one of Herbert's most moving and beautiful poems, the imagery is homely; we find the 'pure, manly, and unaffected' diction which Coleridge noted; the language is simple and direct, and the tone is even. What I wish to stress here is that these qualities of imagery and diction are facets of a much wider and all-embracing quality—the organic unity of the poem, which is concomitant with the oneness of outlook already discussed.

A notable aspect of *The Flower* is the totality of view presented, for Herbert celebrates not only the reawakening, 'the quickning', of the soul, but also the 'killing' which is complementary to it. Throughout, the process is described in terms of flower imagery. The poem begins by celebrating 'thy returns'. The flowers not only have their own intrinsic beauty, the return of God's grace is not only welcome in itself; they are also a happy sign of the passing of winter, the end of spiritual depression:

> How fresh, O Lord, how sweet and clean
> Are thy returns! ev'n as the flowers in spring;
> To which, besides their own demean,
> The late-past frosts tributes of pleasure bring.   (*ll*.1–4)

Herbert extends the flower imagery, comparing his formerly 'shrivel'd heart' to the winter retreat of flowers to their roots. The third stanza is a celebration of this natural order of events:

> These are thy wonders, Lord of power,
> Killing and quickning, bringing down to hell
> And up to heaven in an houre.   (*ll*.15–17)

It is not for man, however, to question the workings of this process, or to ask the reasons:

> We say amisse,
> This or that is:
> Thy word is all, if we could spell.   (*ll*.19–21)

God's word, His ordering of events, *is* all, unchangeably; we would understand this if we could but read, comprehend, that word. The poet then expresses a wish that this state of spiritual revival could be permanent:

> O that I once past changing were,
> Fast in thy Paradise, where no flower can wither!   (*ll*.22–3)

But the thought is immediately followed by a realization that the process of spiritual regeneration is not finite, but a constant striving —'Many a spring I shoot up fair,/Offring at heav'n, growing and groning thither'—and that sin will always have to be combatted, even when man's thoughts are aspiring towards heaven; even in spring there is the 'spring-showre'. There follows a description of the complementary process of spiritual degeneration:

> But while I grow in a straight line,
> Still upwards bent, as if heav'n were mine own,
> Thy anger comes, and I decline.   (ll.29–31)

It is Herbert's spiritual pride and presumption—'as if heav'n were mine own'—which is responsible for God's renewed repression; while man is proud enough in his upward struggle towards heaven to think that heaven is within easy reach, he will continually be put down by God. But the penultimate stanza returns the poet to his former state of grace, and he is, as it were, a new man; 'And now in age I bud again'. The poem's significance is indicated in the final stanza. The purpose of God's 'wonders' of spiritual repression and regeneration is 'To make us see we are but flowers that glide'; when we have the humility to recognize this, to recognize that we are part of His creation, that 'Thy word is all', and that we cannot have presumptuous aspirations to be more what we are, then, and only then, is Paradise assured us. The message is that of the poems already discussed—total dedication and humility before God in an attempt to see His created world aright. In the state of spiritual regeneration created by the coming of God's grace, the poet is able once more to sing his praises: 'I once more smell the dew and rain,/And relish versing'. The concept is reminiscent of those lines in *Love II*:

> Then shall our hearts pant thee; then shall our brain
> All her invention on thine Altar lay,
> And there in hymns send back thy fire again.

The totality of viewpoint in *The Flower* is embodied in imagery conceptually inseparable from the subject-matter. Throughout, the thought of the poem is so naturally evolved from the metaphorical content that the two cannot be divorced. Thus, in the second stanza:

> Who would have thought my shrivel'd heart
> Could have recover'd greennesse?   (ll.8–9)

or again, in the penultimate stanza:

> And now in age I bud again.   (l.36)

25

The metaphors—'my shrivel'd heart', 'recover'd greennesse', 'I bud again'—are simple and direct; but their simplicity and directness derive not merely from the syntax and homeliness, but from their naturalness and inevitability within the context of the poem. Each metaphor is a development of the basic flower imagery, and each is a part, and an extension, of the thought of the poem. This is what I mean by saying the poem is an organic unity. It is the opposite process to seeking out 'quaint words, and trim invention' of which Herbert accused himself in *Jordan* (*II*).

This quality in Herbert's poetry is perhaps best illustrated by a comparison with Donne. Here is the second stanza of *Loves Growth*:

> And yet not greater, but more eminent,
>> Love by the spring is growne;
>> As, in the firmament,
> Starres by the Sunne are not inlarged, but showne.
> Gentle love deeds, as blossomes on a bough,
> From loves awaken'd root do bud out now.
> If, as in water stir'd more circles bee
>> Produc'd by one, love such additions take,
>> Those like to many spheares, but one heaven make,
> For, they are all concentrique unto thee;
> And though each spring doe adde to love new heate,
> As princes doe in times of action get
> New taxes, and remit them not in peace,
> No winter shall abate the spring encrease.

I choose this example merely because it contains imagery superficially similar to that of *The Flower*. Donne, it will be seen, pillages nature; he searches existence around him, the natural world, the universe, for materials which can best be made to express his purpose. The delight of the poem rests not so much in the metaphorical embodiment itself, as in the intellectual processes which that involves. In his *Life of Cowley* Dr. Johnson wrote of the metaphysical poets in general: 'The most heterogeneous ideas are yoked by violence together; nature and art are ransacked for illustrations, comparisons, and allusions.' That well describes Donne's practice, and is the most straightforward definition of the meta-physical 'conceit'. Herbert, in contrast, respects nature, and identifies himself with it. His imagery, unlike Donne's at its most characteristic, is not taken out of the context of the natural order, but is rather an attempt to perceive life within that context. This is why his imagery seldom resembles the metaphysical conceit, and why it seems, not intellectual, but simple, homely, natural.

The organic unity of *The Flower* is a reflection, a poetic re-creation, of the unity of existence which is the theme of the poem. In likening himself to the flower the poet sees himself as an organic part of a universal order in which he firmly believes. There are many references in his poetry to this concept, but one example will suffice; it is where, in *Employment (I)*, Herbert expresses frustration at being outside the order:

> All things are busie; onely I
> Neither bring hony with the bees,
> Nor flowres to make that, nor the husbandrie
> To water these.
>
> I am no link of thy great chain,
> But all my companie is a weed.
> Lord place me in thy consort; give one strain
> To my poore reed.   (*ll*.17–24)

To this search for unity in life, his search to perceive God's created order of existence, Herbert dedicated himself in those poems discussed in part III of the Introduction. This is the search for the essential truth—'Is there in truth no beautie?'—of *Jordan (I)*. It is the search, which we saw in *Dulnesse*, to perceive God in those 'beauties' which are a reflection of His glory. In that poem, so that he might see God, the poet asked Him to 'cleare thy gift, that with a constant wit/I may but look towards thee'. I pointed out his concern was not that 'wit' and 'invention' should disappear from his poetry, but that they should be put to proper use. This is not contradicted by the simplicity and plainness of poems such as *The Flower*. These qualities are a result of the directness of perception Herbert has achieved; underlying the simplicity is a complexity which reflects the complexity of existence itself, of the internal struggles which Herbert endured—'a picture of the many spiritual Conflicts'.

V

The humility and dedication which Herbert applied to his poetry are reflected in the fine workmanship. The astonishing variety of metrical forms in *The Temple*, each one perfected to a high degree, is not just an exhibition of novelty or ingenuity for its own sake; the form is intimately connected with the meaning, and for almost every detail—rhyme-scheme, or broken rhythm, for instance—there is a reason. Even in a poem such as *Easter-wings* (p. 47), which has been regarded by some commentators as no more than an elegant trifle or resourceful diversion, form reinforces meaning. The poem is more than a merely visual attempt to 'imp my wing on thine', for in both stanzas the process of structure reflects the process of thought. In the first, about man's original sin, the full five-foot line is gradually, with the description of the loss of 'wealth and store', whittled down to the two-syllable line, 'Most poore'. When, however, Herbert decides to seek God's aid, and to 'rise' with Him and sing the 'victories' of His Resurrection, the lines regain their full flight. The final line, 'Then shall the fall further the flight in me', indicates the reason for this verse-form: the more his lines contract, the greater will be the 'flight' to their original length. This is an exact parallel to the theological doctrine (see note to *l*.10, p. 129) that the worse the sin the greater the grace, and that because Adam's fall was so great the flight towards God is correspondingly great. The second stanza concerns God's reduction of the individual as punishment for sin: it is through the afflictions visited upon Herbert—when he, and the verse, become 'Most thinne'—that he learns to 'combine' with God in the 'victorie' of the Resurrection; with a corresponding expansion of the verse. Though the immediate subject of the poem is 'the fall of man and his resurrection in Christ' (Joan Bennett), by treating it in this way

28

Herbert has given a peculiarly personal touch; decay and growth, and the regeneration of the individual are subtly made to connect with his efforts and aspirations as poet. And the verse-form is just another aspect of the organic unity already noted.

Evidence that Herbert spent much time polishing and perfecting his poems is provided by the Williams manuscript, in which many alterations have been made in his own hand. Perhaps the most striking example is *The Elixir* (p. 106); several substantial alterations were made to the first version of this famous poem, the most significant being the substitution of the present final stanza for the original:

> But these are high perfections:
> Happy are they that dare
> Lett in the Light to all their actions
> And show them as they are.

Notice how in the new final stanza the introduction of alchemy and the philosopher's stone gives a unity to the whole poem; the concept of the alchemist's search for the essence of things, the elixir, adds point and direction to the first five stanzas, transforming *The Elixir* into a delightfully subtle lyric. The fact that it is so familiar as a hymn should not lead us into disregarding the intricate development of thought so characteristic of Herbert.

Finally, I shall examine a poem which, though on the surface appearing to lack any sort of structure or logical coherence, is perhaps the supreme example of Herbert's powers of organization and perfection. It is the least 'formal' of Herbert's poems, and yet for this very reason it makes the best testimony to his workmanship. What first strikes a reader of *The Collar* (p. 88) is turbulent rebellion represented with dramatic force in haphazard verse form, followed by the poet's final submission to God. And the continual appeal of the poem is that these qualities never lose their force; at each re-reading the rebellion is just as vivid, just as convincing, even though we know that it will be followed by submission.

However, a feeling that the final submission is somehow inevitable points to other aspects of the poem. Implicit in Herbert's description of the rebellion is an element of self-criticism, which is revealed by the structure, verse-form, vocabulary and imagery. However random the train of thought seems to be, however exclamatory the tone, there is a definite line of argument, which clearly divides into four sections: the initial complaint of the heart, the reply that there is 'fruit' if the heart would seek it (beginning *l*.17, 'Not so, my heart'), the heart's complaint repeated and a statement of purpose (*l*.27, 'Away; take heed'), and the final resolution of the conflict in the last four lines. In the verse-form all the elements of order are present, though in a disordered state: although the rhymes appear at haphazard and sometimes distant intervals (e.g. *ll*.3 and 10, *ll*.13 and 23) there is no line of the poem which is unrhymed. Each line contains two, three, four, or five poetic feet, and although randomly arranged these are the basic ingredients for the final regular quatrain of 5, 2, 4 and 3 feet, rhyming *abab*. Notice too how the disorderly imagery of 'double pleasures' has implicit within itself a picture of order: the blood, fruit, wine, crown sequence is the language of Bible and parable, and more particularly recalls the events of the Passion. The vocabulary also hints that Herbert is aware of his shortcomings, as can be seen for instance in the ambiguity implicit in 'good cable' (*l*.24)—'strong cable', 'cable that is good for me'.

Then we come to the four final lines, and the sudden recollection by the reader, with the line 'But as I rav'd and grew more fierce and wilde', that the whole rebellion is a thing of the past, impresses upon us that Herbert has survived and resolved the quarrel within himself. What, then, is the significance of 'Child'? Here again a slight ambiguity enhances the poem's significance. The poet acknowledges his inferiority, God is 'My Lord', the poet is His 'child', and submission is complete ('except ye be as little children, ye shall not enter into the kingdom of heaven'). But 'Child' is also an accusation; Herbert's rebellion, the voice at the end is saying, is essentially childish and foolish. Recognition of this fact is already implicit in the previous lines, which, as we have seen, contain hints of self-criticism. Through a process of self-recognition Herbert has learnt the childishness, the stupidity, of his past behaviour; as a result he has succeeded in resolving the conflict, and has submitted his will, become as a little child, before God.

The Collar demonstrates that Herbert's poetry repays reading and re-reading. The apparent simplicity of many of the poems is their initial virtue; it is what draws us toward them. But even on first acquaintance there is a feeling that this is not all; that underlying the simplicity is a complexity which has been harmonized into finely cadenced verse. To come to terms with that complexity, to realize how Herbert has confronted his internal conflicts, is to gain an appreciation of the unity of outlook which the poems represent. Each poem is, as it were, a reflection of a central spiritual experience from a slightly different angle. The more we read the poems in *The Temple* the more we are able to glimpse of that experience, and to appreciate that Herbert has painted a detailed and complete 'picture of the many spiritual Conflicts'.

SELECT BIBLIOGRAPHY

For editions of Herbert, see Foreword.

BIOGRAPHY

Izaak Walton, *The Life of Mr. George Herbert* (1670); reprinted in Walton's *Lives*, 1670; World's Classics edition (1927).

Margaret Bottrall, *George Herbert*; Murray (1954)—also contains some valuable commentary on the poems.

Marchette Chute, *Two Gentle Men*—biographies of Herbert and Herrick; Secker and Warburg (1960).

CRITICISM

√ S. T. Coleridge, *Biographia Literaria* (1817); chapters 19 and 20.

William Empson, *Seven Types of Ambiguity*; Chatto and Windus (1930).

√ L. C. Knights, 'George Herbert', essay in *Explorations*; Chatto and Windus (1946).

Rosemond Tuve, *A Reading of George Herbert*; Faber and Faber (1952).

Louis L. Martz, *The Poetry of Meditation*; Yale University Press (1954).

Joseph H. Summers, *George Herbert, His Religion and Art*; Chatto and Windus (1954).

Alfred Alvarez, *The School of Donne*; Chatto and Windus (1961).

Joan Bennett, *Five Metaphysical Poets*; Cambridge University Press (1964).

Mary Ellen Rickey, *Utmost Art, Complexity in the Verse of George Herbert*; University of Kentucky Press (1966).

Arnold Stein, *George Herbert's Lyrics*; Johns Hopkins Press (1968).

The Altar

A broken A l t a r, Lord, thy servant reares,
Made of a heart, and cemented with teares:
  Whose parts are as thy hand did frame;
  No workmans tool hath touch'd the same.
          A H e a r t alone   5
          Is   such   a   stone,
          As   nothing   but
          Thy pow'r doth cut.
          Wherefore each part
          Of my hard heart   10
          Meets in this frame,
          To praise thy name.
  That if I chance to hold my peace,
  These stones to praise thee may not cease.
O let thy blessed S a c r i f i c e be mine,   15
And sanctifie this A l t a r to be thine.

The Sacrifice

Oh all ye, who passe by, whose eyes and minde
To worldly things are sharp, but to me blinde;
To me, who took eyes that I might you finde:
                  Was ever grief like mine?

The Princes of my people make a head   5
Against their Maker: they do wish me dead,
Who cannot wish, except I give them bread:
                  Was ever grief like mine?

Without me each one, who doth now me brave,
Had to this day been an Egyptian slave.   10
They use that power against me, which I gave:
                    Was ever grief like mine?

Mine own Apostle, who the bag did beare,
Though he had all I had, did not forbeare
To sell me also, and to put me there: 15
                    Was ever grief like mine?

For thirtie pence he did my death devise,
Who at three hundred did the ointment prize,
Not half so sweet as my sweet sacrifice:
                    Was ever grief like mine?   20

Therefore my soul melts, and my hearts deare treasure
Drops bloud (the onely beads) my words to measure:
O let this cup passe, if it be thy pleasure:
                    Was ever grief like mine?

These drops being temper'd with a sinners tears,   25
A Balsome are for both the Hemispheres:
Curing all wounds, but mine; all, but my fears:
                    Was ever grief like mine?

Yet my Disciples sleep: I cannot gain
One houre of watching; but their drowsie brain   30
Comforts not me, and doth my doctrine stain:
                    Was ever grief like mine?

Arise, arise, they come. Look how they runne.
Alas! what haste they make to be undone!
How with their lanterns do they seek the sunne!   35
                    Was ever grief like mine?

With clubs and staves they seek me, as a thief,
Who am the way & Truth, the true relief;
Most true to those, who are my greatest grief:
                    Was ever grief like mine?   40

Judas, dost thou betray me with a kisse?
Canst thou finde hell about my lips? and misse
Of life, just at the gates of life and blisse?
                    Was ever grief like mine?

See, they lay hold on me, not with the hands   45
Of faith, but furie: yet at their commands
I suffer binding, who have loos'd their bands:
                    Was ever grief like mine?

All my Disciples flie; fear puts a barre
Betwixt my friends and me. They leave the starre,   50
That brought the wise men of the East from farre.
                    Was ever grief like mine?

Then from one ruler to another bound
They leade me; urging, that it was not sound
What I taught: Comments would the text confound.   55
                    Was ever grief like mine?

The Priest and rulers all false witnesse seek
'Gainst him, who seeks not life, but is the meek
And readie Paschal Lambe of this great week:
                    Was ever grief like mine?   60

Then they accuse me of great blasphemie,
That I did thrust into the Deitie,
Who never thought that any robberie:
                    Was ever grief like mine?

Some said, that I the Temple to the floore 65
In three dayes raz'd, and raised as before.
Why, he that built the world can do much more:
                    Was ever grief like mine?

Then they condemne me all with that same breath,
Which I do give them daily, unto death. 70
Thus *Adam* my first breathing rendereth:
                    Was ever grief like mine?

They binde, and leade me unto *Herod:* he
Sends me to *Pilate.* This makes them agree;
But yet their friendship is my enmitie: 75
                    Was ever grief like mine?

Herod and all his bands do set me light,
Who teach all hands to warre, fingers to fight,
And onely am the Lord of Hosts and might:
                    Was ever grief like mine? 80

Herod in judgement sits, while I do stand;
Examines me with a censorious hand:
I him obey, who all things else command:
                    Was ever grief like mine?

The *Jews* accuse me with despitefulnesse; 85
And vying malice with my gentlenesse,
Pick quarrels with their onely happinesse:
                    Was ever grief like mine?

I answer nothing, but with patience prove
If stonie hearts will melt with gentle love. 90
But who does hawk at eagles with a dove?
                    Was ever grief like mine?

My silence rather doth augment their crie;
My dove doth back into my bosome flie,
Because the raging waters still are high: 95
                    Was ever grief like mine?

Heark how they crie aloud still, *Crucifie*:
It is not fit he live a day, they crie,
Who cannot live lesse then eternally:
                    Was ever grief like mine?   100

Pilate a stranger holdeth off; but they,
Mine owne deare people, cry, *Away, away*,
With noises confused frighting the day:
                    Was ever grief like mine?

Yet still they shout, and crie, and stop their eares,   105
Putting my life among their sinnes and fears,
And therefore wish *my bloud on them and theirs:*
                    Was ever grief like mine?

See how spite cankers things. These words aright
Used, and wished, are the whole worlds light: 110
But hony is their gall, brightnesse their night:
                    Was ever grief like mine?

They choose a murderer, and all agree
In him to do themselves a courtesie:
For it was their own cause who killed me: 115
                    Was ever grief like mine?

And a seditious murderer he was:
But I the Prince of peace; peace that doth passe
All understanding, more then heav'n doth glasse:
                    Was ever grief like mine?   120

Why, Caesar is their onely King, not I:
He clave the stonie rock, when they were drie;
But surely not their hearts, as I well trie:
$$\text{Was ever grief like mine?}$$

Ah! how they scourge me! yet my tendernesse   125
Doubles each lash: and yet their bitternesse
Windes up my grief to a mysteriousnesse:
$$\text{Was ever grief like mine?}$$

They buffet him, and box him as they list,
Who grasps the earth and heaven with his fist,   130
And never yet, whom he would punish, miss'd:
$$\text{Was ever grief like mine?}$$

Behold, they spit on me in scornfull wise,
Who by my spittle gave the blinde man eies,
Leaving his blindnesse to mine enemies: 135
$$\text{Was ever grief like mine?}$$

My face they cover, though it be divine.
As *Moses* face was vailed, so is mine,
Lest on their double-dark souls either shine:
$$\text{Was ever grief like mine?} \quad 140$$

Servants and abjects flout me; they are wittie:
Now prophesie who strikes thee, is their dittie.
So they in me denie themselves all pitie:
$$\text{Was ever grief like mine?}$$

And now I am deliver'd unto death,   145
Which each one calls for so with utmost breath,
That he before me well nigh suffereth:
$$\text{Was ever grief like mine?}$$

Weep not, deare friends, since I for both have wept
When all my tears were bloud, the while you slept: 150
Your tears for your own fortunes should be kept:
                Was ever grief like mine?

The souldiers lead me to the common hall;
There they deride me, they abuse me all:
Yet for twelve heav'nly legions I could call: 155
                Was ever grief like mine?

Then with a scarlet robe they me aray;
Which shews my bloud to be the onely way,
And cordiall left to repair mans decay:
                Was ever grief like mine?   160

Then on my head a crown of thorns I wear:
For these are all the grapes *Sion* doth bear,
Though I my vine planted and watred there:
                Was ever grief like mine?

So sits the earths great curse in *Adams* fall   165
Upon my head: so I remove it all
From th' earth unto my brows, and bear the thrall:
                Was ever grief like mine?

Then with the reed they gave to me before,
They strike my head, the rock from whence all store   170
Of heav'nly blessings issue evermore:
                Was ever grief like mine?

They bow their knees to me, and cry, *Hail king:*
What ever scoffes & scornfulnesse can bring,
I am the floore, the sink, where they it fling: 175
                Was ever grief like mine?

Yet since mans scepters are as frail as reeds,
And thorny all their crowns, bloudie their weeds;
I, who am Truth, turn into truth their deeds:
                              Was ever grief like mine?   180

The souldiers also spit upon that face,
Which Angels did desire to have the grace,
And Prophets once to see, but found no place:
                              Was ever grief like mine?

Thus trimmed forth they bring me to the rout,   185
Who *Crucifie him*, crie with one strong shout.
God holds his peace at man, and man cries out:
                              Was ever grief like mine?

They leade me in once more, and putting then
Mine own clothes on, they leade me out agen.   190
Whom devils flie, thus is he toss'd of men:
                              Was ever grief like mine?

And now wearie of sport, glad to ingrosse
All spite in one, counting my life their losse,
They carrie me to my most bitter crosse: 195
                              Was ever grief like mine?

My crosse I bear my self, untill I faint:
Then Simon bears it for me by constraint,
The decreed burden of each mortall Saint:
                              Was ever grief like mine?   200

O all ye who passe by, behold and see;
Man stole the fruit, but I must climbe the tree;
The tree of life to all, but onely me:
                              Was ever grief like mine?

Lo, here I hang, charg'd with a world of sinne,   205
The greater world o' th' two; for that came in
By words, but this by sorrow I must win:
                    Was ever grief like mine?

Such sorrow, as if sinfull man could feel,
Or feel his part, he would not cease to kneel,   210
Till all were melted, though he were all steel:
                    Was ever grief like mine?

But, O *my God, my God!* why leav'st thou me,
The sonne, in whom thou dost delight to be?
My God, my God——   215
                    Never was grief like mine.

Shame tears my soul, my bodie many a wound;
Sharp nails pierce this, but sharper that confound;
Reproches, which are free, while I am bound.
                    Was ever grief like mine?   220

Now heal thy self, Physician; now come down.
Alas! I did so, when I left my crown
And fathers smile for you, to feel his frown:
                    Was ever grief like mine?

In healing not my self, there doth consist   225
All that salvation, which ye now resist;
Your safetie in my sicknesse doth subsist:
                    Was ever grief like mine?

Betwixt two theeves I spend my utmost breath,
As he that for some robberie suffereth.   230
Alas! what have I stollen from you? Death.
                    Was ever grief like mine?

A king my title is, prefixt on high;
Yet by my subjects am condemn'd to die
A servile death in servile companie: 235
                    Was ever grief like mine?

They give me vineger mingled with gall,
But more with malice: yet, when they did call,
With Manna, Angels food, I fed them all:
                    Was ever grief like mine?   240

They part my garments, and by lot dispose
My coat, the type of love, which once cur'd those
Who sought for help, never malicious foes:
                    Was ever grief like mine?

Nay, after death their spite shall further go;   245
For they will pierce my side, I full well know;
That as sinne came, so Sacraments might flow:
                    Was ever grief like mine?

But now I die; now all is finished.
My wo, mans weal: and now I bow my head.   250
Onely let others say, when I am dead,
                    Never was grief like mine.

The Thanksgiving

Oh King of grief! (a title strange, yet true,
    To thee of all kings onely due)
Oh King of wounds! how shall I grieve for thee,
    Who in all grief preventest me?
Shall I weep bloud? why thou hast wept such store   5
    That all thy body was one doore.

Shall I be scourged, flouted, boxed, sold?
    'Tis but to tell the tale is told.
My God, my God, why dost thou part from me?
    Was such a grief as cannot be.   10
Shall I then sing, skipping thy dolefull storie,
    And side with thy triumphant glorie?
Shall thy strokes be my stroking? thorns, my flower?
    Thy rod, my posie? crosse, my bower?
But how then shall I imitate thee, and   15
    Copie thy fair, though bloudie hand?
Surely I will revenge me on thy love,
    And trie who shall victorious prove.
If thou dost give me wealth, I will restore
    All back unto thee by the poore.   20
If thou dost give me honour, men shall see,
    The honour doth belong to thee.
I will not marry; or, if she be mine,
    She and her children shall be thine.
My bosome friend, if he blaspheme thy name,   25
    I will tear thence his love and fame.
One half of me being gone, the rest I give
    Unto some Chappell, die or live.
As for thy passion—But of that anon,
    When with the other I have done.   30
For thy predestination I'le contrive,
    That three yeares hence, if I survive,
I'le build a spittle, or mend common wayes,
    But mend mine own without delayes.
Then I will use the works of thy creation,   35
    As if I us'd them but for fashion.
The world and I will quarrell; and the yeare
    Shall not perceive, that I am here.
My musick shall finde thee, and ev'ry string
    Shall have his attribute to sing;   40

That all together may accord in thee,
    And prove one God, one harmonie.
If thou shalt give me wit, it shall appeare,
    If thou hast giv'n it me, 'tis here.
Nay, I will reade thy book, and never move   45
    Till I have found therein thy love;
Thy art of love, which I'le turn back on thee:
    O my deare Saviour, Victorie!
Then for thy passion—I will do for that—
    Alas, my God, I know not what.   50

The Reprisall

    I HAVE consider'd it, and finde
There is no dealing with thy mighty passion:
For though I die for thee, I am behinde;
    My sinnes deserve the condemnation.

    O make me innocent, that I   5
May give a disentangled state and free:
And yet thy wounds still my attempts defie,
    For by thy death I die for thee.

    Ah! was it not enough that thou
By thy eternall glorie didst outgo me?   10
Couldst thou not griefs sad conquests me allow,
    But in all vict'ries overthrow me?

    Yet by confession will I come
Into thy conquest: though I can do nought
Against thee, in thee I will overcome   15
    The man, who once against thee fought.

The Agonie

PHILOSOPHERS have measur'd mountains,
Fathom'd the depths of seas, of states, and kings,
Walk'd with a staffe to heav'n, and traced fountains:
    But there are two vast, spacious things,
The which to measure it doth more behove: 5
Yet few there are that sound them; Sinne and Love.

    Who would know Sinne, let him repair
Unto mount Olivet; there shall he see
A man so wrung with pains, that all his hair,
    His skinne, his garments bloudie be.   10
Sinne is that presse and vice, which forceth pain
To hunt his cruell food through ev'ry vein.

    Who knows not Love, let him assay
And taste that juice, which on the crosse a pike
Did set again abroach; then let him say   15
    If ever he did taste the like.
Love is that liquor sweet and most divine,
Which my God feels as bloud; but I, as wine.

Redemption

HAVING been tenant long to a rich Lord,
    Not thriving, I resolved to be bold,
    And make a suit unto him, to afford
A new small-rented lease, and cancell th' old.

In heaven at his manour I him sought: 5
    They told me there, that he was lately gone
    About some land, which he had dearly bought
Long since on earth, to take possession.
I straight return'd, and knowing his great birth,
    Sought him accordingly in great resorts;   10
    In cities, theatres, gardens, parks, and courts:
At length I heard a ragged noise and mirth
    Of theeves and murderers: there I him espied,
    Who straight, *Your suit is granted*, said, & died.

Easter

Rise heart; thy Lord is risen. Sing his praise
                Without delayes,
Who takes thee by the hand, that thou likewise
                With him mayst rise:
That, as his death calcined thee to dust,   5
His life may make thee gold, and much more, just.

Awake, my lute, and struggle for thy part
                With all thy art.
The crosse taught all wood to resound his name,
                Who bore the same.   10
His stretched sinews taught all strings, what key
Is best to celebrate this most high day.

Consort both heart and lute, and twist a song
                Pleasant and long:
Or since all musick is but three parts vied   15
                And multiplied

O let thy blessed Spirit bear a part,
And make up our defects with his sweet art.

I got me flowers to straw thy way;
I got me boughs off many a tree: 20
But thou wast up by break of day,
And brought'st thy sweets along with thee.

The Sunne arising in the East,
Though he give light, & th' East perfume;
If they should offer to contest   25
With thy arising, they presume.

Can there be any day but this,
Though many sunnes to shine endeavour?
We count three hundred, but we misse:
There is but one, and that one ever.   30

Easter-wings

LORD, who createdst man in wealth and store,
Though foolishly he lost the same,
Decaying more and more,
Till he became
Most poore: 5
With   thee
O let me rise
As   larks,   harmoniously,
And sing this day thy victories:
Then shall the fall further the flight in me.   10

My tender age in sorrow did beginne:
And still with sicknesses and shame
Thou didst so punish sinne,
That I became
Most thinne.   15
With   thee
Let me combine
And feel this day thy victorie:
For, if I imp my wing on thine,
Affliction shall advance the flight in me.   20

Nature

FULL of rebellion, I would die,
Or fight, or travell, or denie
That thou hast ought to do with me.
                    O tame my heart;
                    It is thy highest art   5
To captivate strong holds to thee.

If thou shalt let his venome lurk,
And in suggestions fume and work,
My soul will turn to bubbles straight,
                    And thence by kinde   10
                    Vanish into a winde,
Making thy workmanship deceit.

O smooth my rugged heart, and there
Engrave thy rev'rend law and fear;
Or make a new one, since the old   15
                    Is saplesse grown,
                    And a much fitter stone
To hide my dust, then thee to hold.

Sinne (I)

Lord, with what care hast thou begirt us round!
    Parents first season us: then schoolmasters
    Deliver us to laws; they send us bound
To rules of reason, holy messengers,
Pulpits and sundayes, sorrow dogging sinne,   5
    Afflictions sorted, anguish of all sizes,
    Fine nets and stratagems to catch us in,
Bibles laid open, millions of surprises,
Blessings beforehand, tyes of gratefulnesse,
    The sound of glorie ringing in our eares: 10
    Without, our shame; within, our consciences;
Angels and grace, eternall hopes and fears.
    Yet all these fences and their whole aray
    One cunning bosome-sinne blows quite away.

Affliction (I)

When first thou didst entice to thee my heart,
                I thought the service brave:
So many joyes I writ down for my part,
                Besides what I might have
Out of my stock of naturall delights,   5
Augmented with thy gracious benefits.

I looked on thy furniture so fine,
                And made it fine to me:
Thy glorious houshold-stuffe did me entwine,
                And 'tice me unto thee.   10
49

Such starres I counted mine: both heav'n and earth
Payd me my wages in a world of mirth.

What pleasures could I want, whose King I served?
                    Where joyes my fellows were.
Thus argu'd into hopes, my thoughts reserved   15
                    No place for grief or fear.
Therefore my sudden soul caught at the place,
And made her youth and fierceness seek thy face.

At first thou gav'st me milk and sweetnesses;
                    I had my wish and way: 20
My dayes were straw'd with flow'rs and happinesse;
                    There was no moneth but May.
But with my yeares sorrow did twist and grow,
And made a partie unawares for wo.

My flesh began unto my soul in pain,   25
                    Sicknesses cleave my bones;
Consuming agues dwell in ev'ry vein,
                    And tune my breath to grones.
Sorrow was all my soul; I scarce beleeved,
Till grief did tell me roundly, that I lived.   30

When I got health, thou took'st away my life,
                    And more; for my friends die:
My mirth and edge was lost; a blunted knife
                    Was of more use then I.
Thus thinne and lean without a fence or friend,   35
I was blown through with ev'ry storm and winde.

Whereas my birth and spirit rather took
                    The way that takes the town;
Thou didst betray me to a lingring book,
                    And wrap me in a gown.   40

I was entangled in the world of strife,
Before I had the power to change my life.

Yet, for I threatned oft the siege to raise,
        Not simpring all mine age,
Thou often didst with Academick praise   45
        Melt and dissolve my rage.
I took thy sweetned pill, till I came where
I could not go away, nor persevere.

Yet lest perchance I should too happie be
        In my unhappinesse,   50
Turning my purge to food, thou throwest me
        Into more sicknesses.
Thus doth thy power crosse-bias me, not making
Thine own gift good, yet me from my wayes taking.

Now I am here, what thou wilt do with me   55
        None of my books will show:
I reade, and sigh, and wish I were a tree;
        For sure then I should grow
To fruit or shade: at least some bird would trust
Her houshold to me, and I should be just.   60

Yet, though thou troublest me, I must be meek;
        In weaknesse must be stout.
Well, I will change the service, and go seek
        Some other master out.
Ah my deare God! though I am clean forgot,   65
Let me not love thee, if I love thee not.

Prayer (I)

PRAYER the Churches banquet, Angels age,
    Gods breath in man returning to his birth,
    The soul in paraphrase, heart in pilgrimage,
The Christian plummet sounding heav'n and earth;
Engine against th' Almightie, sinners towre,   5
    Reversed thunder, Christ-side-piercing spear,
    The six-daies world-transposing in an houre,
A kinde of tune, which all things heare and fear;
Softnesse, and peace, and joy, and love, and blisse,
    Exalted Manna, gladnesse of the best,   10
    Heaven in ordinarie, man well drest,
The milkie way, the bird of Paradise,
    Church-bels beyond the starres heard, the souls bloud,
    The land of spices; something understood.

Antiphon (I)

Cho. LET all the world in ev'ry corner sing,
            My God and King.
    Vers. The heav'ns are not too high,
            His praise may thither flie:
            The earth is not too low,   5
            His praises there may grow.

Cho. Let all the world in ev'ry corner sing,
            My God and King.

Vers. The church with psalms must shout,
No doore can keep them out: 10
But above all, the heart
Must bear the longest part.

Cho. Let all the world in ev'ry corner sing,
My God and King.

Love I

IMMORTALL Love, authour of this great frame,
Sprung from that beautie which can never fade;
How hath man parcel'd out thy glorious name,
And thrown it on that dust which thou hast made,
While mortall love doth all the title gain!   5
Which siding with invention, they together
Bear all the sway, possessing heart and brain,
(Thy workmanship) and give thee share in neither.
Wit fancies beautie, beautie raiseth wit:
The world is theirs; they two play out the game,   10
Thou standing by: and though thy glorious name
Wrought our deliverance from th' infernall pit,
Who sings thy praise? onely a skarf or glove
Doth warm our hands, and make them write of love.

II

IMMORTALL Heat, O let thy greater flame
Attract the lesser to it: let those fires,
Which shall consume the world, first make it tame;
And kindle in our hearts such true desires,

As may consume our lusts, and make thee way.
  Then shall our hearts pant thee; then shall our brain
  All her invention on thine Altar lay,
And there in hymnes send back thy fire again:
Our eies shall see thee, which before saw dust;
  Dust blown by wit, till that they both were blinde: 1
  Thou shalt recover all thy goods in kinde,
Who wert disseized by usurping lust:
  All knees shall bow to thee; all wits shall rise,
  And praise him who did make and mend our eies.

The Temper (I)

How should I praise thee, Lord! how should my rymes
    Gladly engrave thy love in steel,
  If what my soul doth feel sometimes,
    My soul might ever feel!

Although there were some fourtie heav'ns, or more,
    Sometimes I peere above them all;
  Sometimes I hardly reach a score,
    Sometimes to hell I fall.

O rack me not to such a vast extent;
    Those distances belong to thee: 1
  The world's too little for thy tent,
    A grave too big for me.

Wilt thou meet arms with man, that thou dost stretch
    A crumme of dust from heav'n to hell?
  Will great God measure with a wretch?   1
    Shall he thy stature spell?

54

O let me, when thy roof my soul hath hid,
   O let me roost and nestle there:
  Then of a sinner thou art rid,
    And I of hope and fear.   20

Yet take thy way; for sure thy way is best:
   Stretch or contract me, thy poore debter:
  This is but tuning of my breast,
    To make the musick better.

Whether I flie with angels, fall with dust,   25
   Thy hands made both, and I am there:
  Thy power and love, my love and trust
    Make one place ev'ry where.

Jordan (I)

Who sayes that fictions onely and false hair
Become a verse? Is there in truth no beautie?
Is all good structure in a winding stair?
May no lines passe, except they do their dutie
    Not to a true, but painted chair?   5

Is it no verse, except enchanted groves
And sudden arbours shadow course-spunne lines?
Must purling streams refresh a lovers loves?
Must all be vail'd, while he that reades, divines,
    Catching the sense at two removes?   10

Shepherds are honest people; let them sing:
Riddle who list, for me, and pull for Prime:
I envie no mans nightingale or spring;
Nor let them punish me with losse of ryme,
    Who plainly say, *My God, My King*.   15

Employment (I)

IF as a flowre doth spread and die,
    Thou wouldst extend me to some good,
Before I were by frosts extremitie
                Nipt in the bud;

The sweetnesse and the praise were thine;
    But the extension and the room,
Which in thy garland I should fill, were mine
                At thy great doom.

For as thou dost impart thy grace,
    The greater shall our glorie be.
The measure of our joyes is in this place,
                The stuffe with thee.

Let me not languish then, and spend
    A life as barren to thy praise,
As is the dust, to which that life doth tend,
                But with delaies.

All things are busie; onely I
    Neither bring hony with the bees,
Nor flowres to make that, nor the husbandrie
                To water these.

I am no link of thy great chain,
    But all my companie is a weed.
Lord place me in thy consort; give one strain
                To my poore reed.

Church-monuments

WHILE that my soul repairs to her devotion,
Here I intombe my flesh, that it betimes
May take acquaintance of this heap of dust;
To which the blast of deaths incessant motion,
Fed with the exhalation of our crimes,   5
Drives all at last. Therefore I gladly trust
My bodie to this school, that it may learn
To spell his elements, and finde his birth
Written in dustie heraldrie and lines;
Which dissolution sure doth best discern,   10
Comparing dust with dust, and earth with earth.
These laugh at Jeat and Marble put for signes,
To sever the good fellowship of dust,
And spoil the meeting. What shall point out them,
When they shall bow, and kneel, and fall down flat   15
To kisse those heaps, which now they have in trust?
Deare flesh, while I do pray, learn here thy stemme
And true descent; that when thou shalt grow fat,
And wanton in thy cravings, thou mayst know,
That flesh is but the glasse, which holds the dust   20
That measures all our time; which also shall
Be crumbled into dust. Mark here below
How tame these ashes are, how free from lust,
That thou mayst fit thy self against thy fall.

The Church-floore

MARK you the floore? that square & speckled stone,
      Which looks so firm and strong,
         Is *Patience*:

And th' other black and grave, wherewith each one
      Is checker'd all along,   5
         Humilitie:

The gentle rising, which on either hand
      Leads to the Quire above,
         Is *Confidence*:

But the sweet cement, which in one sure band   10
      Ties the whole frame, is *Love*
         And *Charitie*.

      Hither sometimes Sinne steals, and stains
      The marbles neat and curious veins:
But all is cleansed when the marble weeps.   15
      Sometimes Death, puffing at the doore,
      Blows all the dust about the floore:
But while he thinks to spoil the room, he sweeps.
      Blest be the *Architect*, whose art
      Could build so strong in a weak heart.   20

The Windows

Lord, how can man preach thy eternall word?
      He is a brittle crazie glasse:
Yet in thy temple thou dost him afford
        This glorious and transcendent place,
        To be a window, through thy grace.   5

But when thou dost anneal in glasse thy storie,
      Making thy life to shine within
The holy Preachers; then the light and glorie
        More rev'rend grows, & more doth win:
        Which else shows watrish, bleak, & thin.   10

Doctrine and life, colours and light, in one
      When they combine and mingle, bring
A strong regard and aw: but speech alone
        Doth vanish like a flaring thing,
        And in the eare, not conscience ring.   15

Content

Peace mutt'ring thoughts, and do not grudge to keep
      Within the walls of your own breast:
Who cannot on his own bed sweetly sleep,
      Can on anothers hardly rest.

Gad not abroad at ev'ry quest and call   5
      Of an untrained hope or passion.
To court each place or fortune that doth fall,
      Is wantonnesse in contemplation.

Mark how the fire in flints doth quiet lie,
        Content and warm t' it self alone: 10
But when it would appeare to others eye,
        Without a knock it never shone.

Give me the pliant minde, whose gentle measure
        Complies and suits with all estates;
Which can let loose to a crown, and yet with pleasure   15
        Take up within a cloisters gates.

This soul doth span the world, and hang content
        From either pole unto the centre:
Where in each room of the well-furnisht tent
        He lies warm, and without adventure.   20

The brags of life are but a nine dayes wonder;
        And after death the fumes that spring
From private bodies, make as big a thunder,
        As those which rise from a huge King.

Onely thy Chronicle is lost; and yet   25
        Better by worms be all once spent,
Then to have hellish moths still gnaw and fret
        Thy name in books, which may not rent:

When all thy deeds, whose brunt thou feel'st alone,
        Are chaw'd by others pens and tongue;   30
And as their wit is, their digestion,
        Thy nourisht fame is weak or strong.

Then cease discoursing soul, till thine own ground,
        Do not they self or friends importune.
He that by seeking hath himself once found,   35
        Hath ever found a happie fortune.

The Quidditie

MY God, a verse is not a crown,
No point of honour, or gay suit,
No hawk, or banquet, or renown,
Nor a good sword, nor yet a lute:

It cannot vault, or dance, or play;   5
It never was in *France* or *Spain*;
Nor can it entertain the day
With a great stable or demain:

It is no office, art, or news,
Nor the Exchange, or busie Hall;   10
But it is that which while I use
I am with thee, and *Most take all*.

Employment (II)

HE that is weary, let him sit.
          My soul would stirre
And trade in courtesies and wit,
          Quitting the furre
To cold complexions needing it.   5

Man is no starre, but a quick coal
          Of mortall fire:
Who blows it not, nor doth controll
          A faint desire,
Lets his own ashes choke his soul.   10

When th' elements did for place contest
                    With him, whose will
Ordain'd the highest to be best;
                    The earth sat still,
And by the others is opprest.   15

Life is a businesse, not good cheer;
                    Ever in warres.
The sunne still shineth there or here,
                    Whereas the starres
Watch an advantage to appeare.   20

Oh that I were an Orenge-tree,
                    That busie plant!
Then should I ever laden be,
                    And never want
Some fruit for him that dressed me.   25

But we are still too young or old;
                    The Man is gone,
Before we do our wares unfold:
                    So we freeze on,
Untill the grave increase our cold.   30

Deniall

WHEN my devotions could not pierce
                    Thy silent eares;
Then was my heart broken, as was my verse:
          My breast was full of fears
                    And disorder: 5

62

My bent thoughts, like a brittle bow,
$$\qquad\qquad$$ Did flie asunder:
Each took his way; some would to pleasures go,
$$\qquad$$ Some to the warres and thunder
$$\qquad\qquad\qquad$$ Of alarms. $\qquad$ 10

As good go any where, they say,
$$\qquad\qquad$$ As to benumme
Both knees and heart, in crying night and day,
$$\qquad$$ *Come, come, my God, O come,*
$$\qquad\qquad\qquad$$ But no hearing. $\qquad$ 15

O that thou shouldst give dust a tongue
$$\qquad\qquad$$ To crie to thee,
And then not heare it crying! all day long
$$\qquad$$ My heart was in my knee,
$$\qquad\qquad\qquad$$ But no hearing. $\qquad$ 20

Therefore my soul lay out of sight,
$$\qquad\qquad$$ Untun'd, unstrung:
My feeble spirit, unable to look right,
$$\qquad$$ Like a nipt blossome, hung
$$\qquad\qquad\qquad$$ Discontented. $\qquad$ 25

O cheer and tune my heartlesse breast,
$$\qquad\qquad$$ Deferre no time;
That so thy favours granting my request,
$$\qquad$$ They and my minde may chime,
$$\qquad\qquad\qquad$$ And mend my ryme. $\qquad$ 30

Vanitie (I)

THE fleet Astronomer can bore,
And thred the spheres with his quick-piercing minde:
He views their stations, walks from doore to doore,
    Surveys, as if he had design'd
To make a purchase there: he sees their dances,   5
           And knoweth long before,
Both their full-ey'd aspects, and secret glances.

The nimble Diver with his side
Cuts through the working waves, that he may fetch
His dearely-earned pearl, which God did hide   10
    On purpose from the ventrous wretch;
That he might save his life, and also hers,
           Who with excessive pride
Her own destruction and his danger wears.

The subtil Chymick can devest   15
And strip the creature naked, till he finde
The callow principles within their nest:
    There he imparts to them his minde,
Admitted to their bed-chamber, before
           They appeare trim and drest   20
To ordinarie suitours at the doore.

What hath not man sought out and found,
But his deare God? who yet his glorious law
Embosomes in us, mellowing the ground
    With showres and frosts, with love & aw,   25
So that we need not say, Where's this command?
           Poore man, thou searchest round
To finde out *death*, but missest *life* at hand.

Vertue

SWEET day, so cool, so calm, so bright,
The bridall of the earth and skie:
The dew shall weep thy fall to night;
           For thou must die.

Sweet rose, whose hue angrie and brave   5
Bids the rash gazer wipe his eye:
Thy root is ever in its grave,
           And thou must die.

Sweet spring, full of sweet dayes and roses,
A box where sweets compacted lie;   10
My musick shows ye have your closes,
           And all must die.

Onely a sweet and vertuous soul,
Like season'd timber, never gives;
But though the whole world turn to coal,   15
           Then chiefly lives.

The Pearl

I KNOW the wayes of learning; both the head
And pipes that feed the presse, and make it runne;
What reason hath from nature borrowed,
Or of it self, like a good huswife, spunne
In laws and policie; what the starres conspire,   5
What willing nature speaks, what forc'd by fire;
Both th' old discoveries, and the new-found seas,

The stock and surplus, cause and historie:
All these stand open, or I have the keyes:
                              Yet I love thee.   10

I know the wayes of honour, what maintains
The quick returns of courtesie and wit:
In vies of favours whether partie gains,
When glorie swells the heart, and moldeth it
To all expressions both of hand and eye,   15
Which on the world a true-love-knot may tie,
And bear the bundle, wheresoe're it goes:
How many drammes of spirit there must be
To sell my life unto my friends or foes:
                              Yet I love thee.   20

I know the wayes of pleasure, the sweet strains,
The lullings and the relishes of it;
The propositions of hot bloud and brains;
What mirth and musick mean; what love and wit
Have done these twentie hundred yeares, and more: 25
I know the projects of unbridled store:
My stuffe is flesh, not brasse; my senses live,
And grumble oft, that they have more in me
Then he that curbs them, being but one to five:
                              Yet I love thee.   30

I know all these, and have them in my hand:
Therefore not sealed, but with open eyes
I flie to thee, and fully understand
Both the main sale, and the commodities;
And at what rate and price I have thy love;   35
With all the circumstances that may move:
Yet through these labyrinths, not my groveling wit,
But thy silk twist let down from heav'n to me,
Did both conduct and teach me, how by it
                              To climbe to thee.   40

Affliction (IV)

BROKEN in pieces all asunder,
      Lord, hunt me not,
      A thing forgot,
Once a poore creature, now a wonder,
      A wonder tortur'd in the space   5
      Betwixt this world and that of grace.

My thoughts are all a case of knives,
      Wounding my heart
      With scatter'd smart,
As watring pots give flowers their lives.   10
      Nothing their furie can controll,
      While they do wound and pink my soul.

All my attendants are at strife,
      Quitting their place
      Unto my face: 15
Nothing performs the task of life:
      The elements are let loose to fight,
      And while I live, trie out their right.

Oh help, my God! let not their plot
      Kill them and me,   20
      And also thee,
Who art my life: dissolve the knot,
      As the sunne scatters by his light
      All the rebellions of the night.

Then shall those powers, which work for grief,   25
    Enter thy pay,
    And day by day
Labour thy praise, and my relief;
    With care and courage building me,
    Till I reach heav'n, and much more, thee.   30

Man

MY God, I heard this day,
That none doth build a stately habitation,
    But he that means to dwell therein.
    What house more stately hath there been,
Or can be, then is Man? to whose creation   5
    All things are in decay.

    For Man is ev'ry thing,
And more: He is a tree, yet bears more fruit;
    A beast, yet is, or should be more:
    Reason and speech we onely bring.   10
Parrats may thank us, if they are not mute,
    They go upon the score.

    Man is all symmetrie,
Full of proportions, one limbe to another,
    And all to all the world besides: 15
    Each part may call the farthest, brother:
For head with foot hath private amitie,
    And both with moons and tides.

    Nothing hath got so farre,
But Man hath caught and kept it, as his prey.   20
    His eyes dismount the highest starre:
    He is in little all the sphere.

Herbs gladly cure our flesh; because that they
    Finde their acquaintance there.

    For us the windes do blow,   25
The earth doth rest, heav'n move, and fountains flow.
    Nothing we see, but means our good,
    As our *delight*, or as our *treasure*:
The whole is, either our cupboard of *food*,
    Or cabinet of *pleasure*.   30

    The starres have us to bed;
Night draws the curtain, which the sunne withdraws;
    Musick and light attend our head.
    All things unto our *flesh* are kinde
In their *descent* and *being*; to our *minde*   35
    In their *ascent* and *cause*.

    Each thing is full of dutie:
Waters united are our navigation;
    Distinguished, our habitation;
    Below, our drink; above, our meat;   40
Both are our cleanlinesse. Hath one such beautie?
    Then how are all things neat?

    More servants wait on Man,
Then he'l take notice of: in ev'ry path
    He treads down that which doth befriend him,   45
    When sicknesse makes him pale and wan.
Oh mightie love! Man is one world, and hath
    Another to attend him.

    Since then, my God, thou hast
So brave a Palace built; O dwell in it,   50
    That it may dwell with thee at last!
    Till then, afford us so much wit;
That, as the world serves us, we may serve thee,
    And both thy servants be.

Life

I MADE a posie, while the day ran by:
Here will I smell my remnant out, and tie
        My life within this band.
But time did becken to the flowers, and they
By noon most cunningly did steal away,
        And wither'd in my hand.

My hand was next to them, and then my heart:
I took, without more thinking, in good part
        Times gentle admonition:
Who did so sweetly deaths sad taste convey,
Making my minde to smell my fatall day;
        Yet sugring the suspicion.

Farewell deare flowers, sweetly your time ye spent,
Fit, while ye liv'd, for smell or ornament,
        And after death for cures.
I follow straight without complaints or grief,
Since if my sent be good, I care not, if
        It be as short as yours.

Affliction (V)

My God, I read this day,
That planted Paradise was not so firm,
As was and is thy floting Ark; whose stay
And anchor thou art onely, to confirm
    And strengthen it in ev'ry age,
  When waves do rise, and tempests rage.

At first we liv'd in pleasure;
Thine own delights thou didst to us impart:
When we grew wanton, thou didst use displeasure
To make us thine: yet that we might not part,   10
    As we at first did board with thee,
    Now thou wouldst taste our miserie.

There is but joy and grief;
If either will convert us, we are thine:
Some Angels us'd the first; if our relief   15
Take up the second, then thy double line
    And sev'rall baits in either kinde
    Furnish thy table to thy minde.

Affliction then is ours;
We are the trees, whom shaking fastens more,   20
While blustring windes destroy the wanton bowres,
And ruffle all their curious knots and store.
    My God, so temper joy and wo,
    That thy bright beams may tame thy bow.

Mortification

How soon doth man decay!
When clothes are taken from a chest of sweets
To swaddle infants, whose young breath
    Scarce knows the way;
Those clouts are little winding sheets,   5
Which do consigne and send them unto death.

71

When boyes go first to bed,
They step into their voluntarie graves,
Sleep bindes them fast; onely their breath
Makes them not dead: 10
Successive nights, like rolling waves,
Convey them quickly, who are bound for death.

When youth is frank and free,
And calls for musick, while his veins do swell,
All day exchanging mirth and breath   15
In companie;
That musick summons to the knell,
Which shall befriend him at the houre of death.

When man grows staid and wise,
Getting a house and home, where he may move   20
Within the circle of his breath,
Schooling his eyes;
That dumbe inclosure maketh love
Unto the coffin, that attends his death.

When age grows low and weak,   25
Marking his grave, and thawing ev'ry yeare,
Till all do melt, and drown his breath
When he would speak;
A chair or litter shows the biere,
Which shall convey him to the house of death.   30

Man, ere he is aware,
Hath put together a solemnitie,
And drest his herse, while he has breath
As yet to spare:
Yet Lord, instruct us so to die,   35
That all these dyings may be life in death.

Decay

Sᴡᴇᴇᴛ were the dayes, when thou didst lodge with Lot,
Struggle with Jacob, sit with Gideon,
Advise with Abraham, when thy power could not
Encounter Moses strong complaints and mone:
    Thy words were then, *Let me alone.* 5

One might have sought and found thee presently
At some fair oak, or bush, or cave, or well:
Is my God this way? No, they would reply:
He is to Sinai gone, as we heard tell:
    List, ye may heare great Aarons bell. 10

But now thou dost thy self immure and close
In some one corner of a feeble heart:
Where yet both Sinne and Satan, thy old foes,
Do pinch and straiten thee, and use much art
    To gain thy thirds and little part. 15

I see the world grows old, when as the heat
Of thy great love once spread, as in an urn
Doth closet up it self, and still retreat,
Cold sinne still forcing it, till it return,
    And calling Justice, all things burn. 20

Jordan (II)

Wʜᴇɴ first my lines of heav'nly joyes made mention,
Such was their lustre, they did so excell,
That I sought out quaint words, and trim invention;

My thoughts began to burnish, sprout, and swell,
Curling with metaphors a plain intention,   5
Decking the sense, as if it were to sell.

Thousands of notions in my brain did runne,
Off'ring their service, if I were not sped:
I often blotted what I had begunne;
This was not quick enough, and that was dead.   10
Nothing could seem too rich to clothe the sunne,
Much lesse those joyes which trample on his head.

As flames do work and winde, when they ascend,
So did I weave my self into the sense.
But while I bustled, I might heare a friend   15
Whisper, *How wide is all this long pretence!*
There is in love a sweetnesse readie penn'd:
Copie out onely that, and save expense.

Conscience

PEACE pratler, do not lowre:
Not a fair look, but thou dost call it foul:
Not a sweet dish, but thou dost call it sowre:
    Musick to thee doth howl.
  By listning to thy chatting fears   5
  I have both lost mine eyes and eares.

Pratler, no more, I say:
My thoughts must work, but like a noiselesse sphere;
Harmonious peace must rock them all the day:
    No room for pratlers there.   10
  If thou persistest, I will tell thee,
  That I have physick to expell thee.

And the receit shall be
My Saviours bloud: when ever at his board
I do but taste it, straight it cleanseth me,   15
    And leaves thee not a word;
  No, not a tooth or nail to scratch,
  And at my actions carp, or catch.

    Yet if thou talkest still,
Besides my physick, know there's some for thee: 20
Some wood and nails to make a staffe or bill
    For those that trouble me:
  The bloudie crosse of my deare Lord
  Is both my physick and my sword.

The Quip

THE merrie world did on a day
With his train-bands and mates agree
To meet together, where I lay,
And all in sport to geere at me.

First, Beautie crept into a rose,   5
Which when I pluckt not, Sir, said she,
Tell me, I pray, Whose hands are those?
But thou shalt answer, Lord, for me.

Then Money came, and chinking still,
What tune is this, poore man? said he: 10
I heard in Musick you had skill.
But thou shalt answer, Lord, for me.

Then came brave Glorie puffing by
In silks that whistled, who but he?
He scarce allow'd me half an eie.   15
But thou shalt answer, Lord, for me.

Then came quick Wit and Conversation,
And he would needs a comfort be,
And, to be short, make an Oration.
But thou shalt answer, Lord, for me.   20

Yet when the houre of they designe
To answer these fine things shall come;
Speak not at large; say, I am thine:
And then they have their answer home.

Dialogue

Sweetest Saviour, if my soul
      Were but worth the having,
Quickly should I then controll
      Any thought of waving.
But when all my care and pains   5
Cannot give the name of gains
To thy wretch so full of stains;
What delight or hope remains?

What (childe) is the ballance thine,
      Thine the poise and measure?   10
If I say, Thou shalt be mine;
      Finger not my treasure.
What the gains in having thee
Do amount to, onely he,
Who for man was sold, can see;   15
That transferr'd th' accounts to me.

But as I can see no merit,
    Leading to this favour:
So the way to fit me for it,
    Is beyond my savour.   20
As the reason then is thine;
So the way is none of mine:
I disclaim the whole designe:
Sinne disclaims and I resigne.

That is all, if that I could   25
    Get without repining;
And my clay, my creature would
    Follow my resigning.
That as I did freely part
With my glorie and desert,   30
Left all joyes to feel all smart— —
    Ah! no more: thou break'st my heart.

Dulnesse

Why do I languish thus, drooping and dull,
    As if I were all earth?
O give me quicknesse, that I may with mirth
        Praise thee brim-full!

The wanton lover in a curious strain   5
    Can praise his fairest fair;
And with quaint metaphors her curled hair
        Curl o're again.

Thou art my lovelinesse, my life, my light,
    Beautie alone to me: 10
Thy bloudy death and undeserv'd, makes thee
        Pure red and white.

When all perfections as but one appeare,
    That those thy form doth show,
The very dust, where thou dost tread and go,   15
             Makes beauties here;

Where are my lines then? my approaches? views?
    Where are my window-songs?
Lovers are still pretending, & ev'n wrongs
          Sharpen their Muse: 20

But I am lost in flesh, whose sugred lyes
    Still mock me, and grow bold:
Sure thou didst put a minde there, if I could
          Finde where it lies.

Lord, cleare thy gift, that with a constant wit   25
    I may but look towards thee:
Look onely; for to *love* thee, who can be,
          What angel fit?

Hope

I GAVE to Hope a watch of mine: but he
          An anchor gave to me.
Then an old prayer-book I did present:
          And he an optick sent.
With that I gave a viall full of tears: 5
          But he a few green eares:
Ah Loyterer! I'le no more, no more I'le bring:
          I did expect a ring.

Sinnes round

SORRIE I am, my God, sorrie I am,
That my offences course it in a ring.
My thoughts are working like a busie flame,
Untill their cockatrice they hatch and bring:
And when they once have perfected their draughts,   5
My words take fire from my inflamed thoughts.

My words take fire from my inflamed thoughts,
Which spit it forth like the Sicilian hill.
They vent the wares, and passe them with their faults,
And by their breathing ventilate the ill.   10
But words suffice not, where are lewd intentions:
My hands do joyn to finish the inventions.

My hands do joyn to finish the inventions:
And so my sinnes ascend three stories high,
As Babel grew, before there were dissensions.   15
Yet ill deeds loyter not: for they supplie
New thoughts of sinning: wherefore, to my shame,
Sorrie I am, my God, sorrie I am.

Confession

O WHAT a cunning guest
Is this same grief! within my heart I made
    Closets; and in them many a chest;
    And like a master in my trade,
In those chests, boxes; in each box, a till: 5
Yet grief knows all, and enters when he will.

79

No scrue, no piercer can
Into a piece of timber work and winde,
    As Gods afflictions into man,
    When he a torture hath design'd.   10
They are too subtill for the subt'llest hearts;
And fall, like rheumes, upon the tendrest parts.

        We are the earth; and they,
Like moles within us, heave, and cast about:
    And till they foot and clutch their prey,   15
    They never cool, much lesse give out.
No smith can make such locks, but they have keyes:
Closets are halls to them; and hearts, high-wayes.

        Onely an open breast
Doth shut them out, so that they cannot enter;   20
    Or, if they enter, cannot rest,
    But quickly seek some new adventure.
Smooth open hearts no fastning have; but fiction
Doth give a hold and handle to affliction.

        Wherefore my faults and sinnes,   25
Lord, I acknowledge; take thy plagues away:
    For since confession pardon winnes,
    I challenge here the brightest day,
The clearest diamond: let them do their best,
They shall be thick and cloudie to my breast.   30

Giddinesse

OH, what a thing is man! how farre from power,
    From setled peace and rest!
He is some twentie sev'rall men at least
    Each sev'rall houre.

One while he counts of heav'n, as of his treasure: 5
    But then a thought creeps in,
And calls him coward, who for fear of sinne
    Will lose a pleasure.

Now he will fight it out, and to the warres;
    Now eat his bread in peace,   10
And snudge in quiet: now he scorns increase;
    Now all day spares.

He builds a house, which quickly down must go,
    As if a whirlwinde blew
And crusht the building: and it's partly true,   15
    His minde is so.

O what a sight were Man, if his attires
    Did alter with his minde;
And like a Dolphins skinne, his clothes combin'd
    With his desires!   20

Surely if each one saw anothers heart,
    There would be no commerce,
No sale or bargain passe: all would disperse,
    And live apart.

Lord, mend or rather make us: one creation   25
    Will not suffice our turn:
Except thou make us dayly, we shall spurn
    Our own salvation.

The Bunch of Grapes

Joy, I did lock thee up: but some bad man
        Hath let thee out again:
And now, me thinks, I am where I began
        Sev'n yeares ago: one vogue and vein,
        One aire of thoughts usurps my brain.   5
I did toward Canaan draw; but now I am
Brought back to the Red sea, the sea of shame.

For as the Jews of old by Gods command
        Travell'd, and saw no town:
So now each Christian hath his journeys spann'd: 10
        Their storie pennes and sets us down.
        A single deed is small renown.
Gods works are wide, and let in future times;
His ancient justice overflows our crimes.

Then have we too our guardian fires and clouds;   15
        Our Scripture-dew drops fast:
We have our sands and serpents, tents and shrowds;
        Alas! our murmurings come not last.
        But where's the cluster? where's the taste
Of mine inheritance? Lord, if I must borrow,   20
Let me as well take up their joy, as sorrow.

But can he want the grape, who hath the wine?
        I have their fruit and more.
Blessed be God, who prosper'd *Noahs* vine,
        And made it bring forth grapes good store.   25
        But much more him I must adore,
Who of the laws sowre juice sweet wine did make,
Ev'n God himself being pressed for my sake.

Mans medley

HEARK, how the birds do sing,
　　And woods do ring.
All creatures have their joy: and man hath his.
　　Yet if we rightly measure,
　　Mans joy and pleasure
Rather hereafter, then in present, is.

　　To this life things of sense
　　Make their pretence:
In th' other Angels have a right by birth:
　　Man ties them both alone,
　　And makes them one,
With th' one hand touching heav'n, with th' other earth.

　　In soul he mounts and flies,
　　In flesh he dies.
He wears a stuffe whose thread is course and round,
　　But trimm'd with curious lace,
　　And should take place
After the trimming, not the stuffe and ground.

　　Not, that he may not here
　　Taste of the cheer,
But as birds drink, and straight lift up their head,
　　So must he sip and think
　　Of better drink
He may attain to, after he is dead.

　　But as his joyes are double;
　　So is his trouble.

He hath two winters, other things but one:
    Both frosts and thoughts do nip,
      And bite his lip;
And he of all things fears two deaths alone.   30

    Yet ev'n the greatest griefs
      May be reliefs,
Could he but take them right, and in their wayes.
    Happie is he, whose heart
      Hath found the art   35
To turn his double pains to double praise.

Divinitie

As men, for fear the starres should sleep and nod,
    And trip at night, have spheres suppli'd;
As if a starre were duller then a clod,
    Which knows his way without a guide:

Just so the other heav'n they also serve,   5
    Divinities transcendent skie:
Which with the edge of wit they cut and carve.
    Reason triumphs, and faith lies by.

Could not that wisdome, which first broacht the wine,
    Have thicken'd it with definitions?   10
And jagg'd his seamlesse coat, had that been fine,
    With curious questions and divisions?

But all the doctrine, which he taught and gave,
    Was cleare as heav'n, from whence it came.
At least those beams of truth, which onely save,   15
    Surpasse in brightnesse any flame.

Love God, and love your neighbour. Watch and pray.
    Do as ye would be done unto.
O dark instructions; ev'n as dark as day!
    Who can these Gordian knots undo?   20

But he doth bid us take his bloud for wine.
    Bid what he please; yet I am sure,
To take and taste what he doth there designe,
    Is all that saves, and not obscure.

Then burn thy Epicycles, foolish man;   25
    Break all thy spheres, and save thy head.
Faith needs no staffe of flesh, but stoutly can
    To heav'n alone both go, and leade.

The Pilgrimage

I TRAVELL'D on, seeing the hill, where lay
              My expectation.
    A long it was and weary way.
    The gloomy cave of Desperation
I left on th' one, and on the other side   5
              The rock of Pride.

And so I came to Fancies medow strow'd
              With many a flower:
    Fain would I here have made abode,
    But I was quicken'd by my houre.   10
So to Cares cops I came, and there got through
              With much ado.

That led me to the wilde of Passion, which
                    Some call the wold;
    A wasted place, but sometimes rich.   1
    Here I was robb'd of all my gold,
Save one good Angell, which a friend had ti'd
                    Close to my side.

At length I got unto the gladsome hill,
                    Where lay my hope,   2(
    Where lay my heart; and climbing still,
    When I had gain'd the brow and top,
A lake of brackish waters on the ground
                    Was all I found.

With that abash'd and struck with many a sting   2
                    Of swarming fears,
    I fell, and cry'd, Alas my King;
    Can both the way and end be tears?
Yet taking heart I rose, and then perceiv'd
                    I was deceiv'd: 3(

My hill was further: so I flung away,
                    Yet heard a crie
    Just as I went, *None goes that way*
    And lives: If that be all, said I,
After so foul a journey death is fair,   3
                    And but a chair.

The Holdfast

I THREATNED to observe the strict decree
    Of my deare God with all my power & might.
    But I was told by one, it could not be;

Yet I might trust in God to be my light.
Then will I trust, said I, in him alone.   5
  Nay, ev'n to trust in him, was also his:
  We must confesse, that nothing is our own.
Then I confesse that he my succour is:
But to have nought is ours, not to confesse
  That we have nought. I stood amaz'd at this,   10
  Much troubled, till I heard a friend expresse,
That all things were more ours by being his.
  What Adam had, and forfeited for all,
  Christ keepeth now, who cannot fail or fall.

Praise (II)

KING of Glorie, King of Peace,
    I will love thee:
And that love may never cease,
    I will move thee.

Thou hast granted my request,   5
    Thou hast heard me:
Thou didst note my working breast,
    Thou hast spar'd me.

Wherefore with my utmost art
    I will sing thee,   10
And the cream of all my heart
    I will bring thee.

Though my sinnes against me cried,
    Thou didst cleare me;
And alone, when they replied,   15
    Thou didst heare me.

Sev'n whole dayes, not one in seven,
        I will praise thee.
In my heart, though not in heaven,
        I can raise thee. 20

Thou grew'st soft and moist with tears,
        Thou relentedst:
And when Justice call'd for fears,
        Thou dissentedst.

Small it is, in this poore sort 25
        To enroll thee:
Ev'n eternitie is too short
        To extoll thee.

The Collar

I STRUCK the board, and cry'd, No more.
        I will abroad.
What? shall I ever sigh and pine?
My lines and life are free: free as the rode,
    Loose as the winde, as large as store. 5
        Shall I be still in suit?
Have I no harvest but a thorn
To let me bloud, and not restore
What I have lost with cordiall fruit?
        Sure there was wine 10
Before my sighs did drie it: there was corn
        Before my tears did drown it.
Is the yeare onely lost to me?
        Have I no bayes to crown it?

No flowers, no garlands gay? all blasted?   15
          All wasted?
    Not so, my heart: but there is fruit,
          And thou hast hands.
    Recover all thy sigh-blown age
On double pleasures: leave thy cold dispute   20
Of what is fit, and not. Forsake thy cage,
          Thy rope of sands,
Which pettie thoughts have made, and made to thee
    Good cable, to enforce and draw,
          And be thy law,   25
    While thou didst wink and wouldst not see.
          Away; take heed:
          I will abroad.
Call in thy deaths head there: tie up thy fears.
          He that forbears   30
          To suit and serve his need,
          Deserves his load.
But as I rav'd and grew more fierce and wilde
          At every word,
Me thoughts I heard one calling, *Child!*   35
          And I reply'd, *My Lord.*

The Glimpse

WHITHER away delight?
Thou cam'st but now; wilt thou so soon depart,
          And give me up to night?
For many weeks of lingring pain and smart
But one half houre of comfort for my heart?   5

Me thinks delight should have
More skill in musick, and keep better time.
    Wert thou a winde or wave,
They quickly go and come with lesser crime:
Flowers look about, and die not in their prime.   10

    Thy short abode and stay
Feeds not, but addes to the desire of meat.
    Lime begg'd of old (they say)
A neighbour spring to cool his inward heat;
Which by the springs accesse grew much more great.   15

    In hope of thee my heart
Pickt here and there a crumme, and would not die;
    But constant to his part
When as my fears foretold this, did replie,
A slender thread a gentle guest will tie.   20

    Yet if the heart that wept
Must let thee go, return when it doth knock.
    Although thy heap be kept
For future times, the droppings of the stock
May oft break forth, and never break the lock.   25

    If I have more to spinne,
The wheel shall go, so that thy stay be short.
    Thou knowst how grief and sinne
Disturb the work. O make me not their sport,
Who by thy coming may be made a court!   30

Clasping of hands

LORD, thou art mine, and I am thine,
If mine I am: and thine much more,
Then I or ought, or can be mine.
Yet to be thine, doth me restore;
So that again I now am mine,   5
And with advantage mine the more
Since this being mine, brings with it thine,
And thou with me dost thee restore.
    If I without thee would be mine,
    I neither should be mine nor thine.   10

Lord, I am thine, and thou art mine:
So mine thou art, that something more
I may presume thee mine, then thine.
For thou didst suffer to restore
Not thee, but me, and to be mine: 15
And with advantage mine the more,
Since thou in death wast none of thine,
Yet then as mine didst me restore.
    O be mine still! still make me thine!
    Or rather make no Thine and Mine!   20

Josephs coat

WOUNDED I sing, tormented I indite,
Thrown down I fall into a bed, and rest:
Sorrow hath chang'd its note: such is his will,

Who changeth all things, as him pleaseth best.
　　For well he knows, if but one grief and smart　　5
Among my many had his full career,
Sure it would carrie with it ev'n my heart,
And both would runne untill they found a biere
　　To fetch the bodie; both being due to grief.
But he hath spoil'd the race; and giv'n to anguish　　10
One of Joyes coats, ticing it with relief
To linger in me, and together languish.
　　I live to shew his power, who once did bring
　　My *joyes* to *weep*, and now my *griefs* to *sing*.

The Pulley

Wʜᴇɴ God at first made man,
Having a glasse of blessings standing by;
Let us (said he) poure on him all we can:
Let the worlds riches, which dispersed lie,
　　Contract into a span.　　5

So strength first made a way;
Then beautie flow'd, then wisdome, honour, pleasure:
When almost all was out, God made a stay,
Perceiving that alone of all his treasure
　　Rest in the bottome lay.　　10

For if I should (said he)
Bestow this jewell also on my creature,
He would adore my gifts in stead of me,
And rest in Nature, not the God of Nature:
　　So both should losers be.　　15

Yet let him keep the rest,
But keep them with repining restlesnesse:
Let him be rich and wearie, that at least,
If goodnesse leade him not, yet wearinesse
    May tosse him to my breast.   20

The Priesthood

Blest Order, which in power dost so excell,
That with th' one hand thou liftest to the sky,
And with the other throwest down to hell
In thy just censures; fain would I draw nigh,
Fain put thee on, exchanging my lay-sword   5
        For that of th' holy word.

But thou art fire, sacred and hallow'd fire;
And I but earth and clay: should I presume
To wear thy habit, the severe attire
My slender compositions might consume.   10
I am both foul and brittle; much unfit
        To deal in holy Writ.

Yet have I often seen, by cunning hand
And force of fire, what curious things are made
Of wretched earth. Where once I scorn'd to stand, 15
That earth is fitted by the fire and trade
Of skilfull artists, for the boards of those
        Who make the bravest shows.

But since those great ones, be they ne're so great,
Come from the earth, from whence those vessels come; 20
So that at once both feeder, dish, and meat

Have one beginning and one finall summe:
I do not greatly wonder at the sight,
                If earth in earth delight.

But th' holy men of God such vessels are,   25
As serve him up, who all the world commands:
When God vouchsafeth to become our fare,
Their hands convey him, who conveys their hands.
O what pure things, most pure must those things be,
              Who bring my God to me!   30

Wherefore I dare not, I, put forth my hand
To hold the Ark, although it seem to shake
Through th' old sinnes and new doctrines of our land.
Onely, since God doth often vessels make
Of lowly matter for high uses meet,   35
              I throw me at his feet.

There will I lie, untill my Maker seek
For some mean stuffe whereon to show his skill:
Then is my time. The distance of the meek
Doth flatter power. Lest good come short of ill   40
In praising might, the poore do by submission
              What pride by opposition.

Grief

O WHO will give me tears? Come all ye springs,
  Dwell in my head & eyes: come clouds, & rain:
My grief hath need of all the watry things,
  That nature hath produc'd. Let ev'ry vein
Suck up a river to supply mine eyes,   5
  My weary weeping eyes too drie for me,

Unlesse they get new conduits, new supplies
To bear them out, and with my state agree.
What are two shallow foords, two little spouts
Of a lesse world? the greater is but small,   10
A narrow cupboard for my griefs and doubts,
Which want provision in the midst of all.
Verses, ye are too fine a thing, too wise
For my rough sorrows: cease, be dumbe and mute,
Give up your feet and running to mine eyes,   15
And keep your measures for some lovers lute,
Whose grief allows him musick and a ryme:
For mine excludes both measure, tune, and time.
                    Alas, my God!

The Crosse

WHAT is this strange and uncouth thing?
To make me sigh, and seek, and faint, and die,
Untill I had some place, where I might sing,
        And serve thee; and not onely I,
But all my wealth and familie might combine   5
To set thy honour up, as our designe.

    And then when after much delay,
Much wrastling, many a combate, this deare end,
So much desir'd, is giv'n, to take away
        My power to serve thee; to unbend   10
All my abilities, my designes confound,
And lay my threatnings bleeding on the ground.

    One ague dwelleth in my bones,
Another in my soul (the memorie

What I would do for thee, if once my grones   15
    Could be allow'd for harmonie):
I am in all a weak disabled thing,
Save in the sight thereof, where strength doth sting.

    Besides, things sort not to my will,
Ev'n when my will doth studie thy renown: 20
Thou turnest th' edge of all things on me still,
    Taking me up to throw me down:
So that, ev'n when my hopes seem to be sped,
I am to grief alive, to them as dead.

    To have my aim, and yet to be   25
Farther from it then when I bent my bow;
To make my hopes my torture, and the fee
    Of all my woes another wo,
Is in the midst of delicates to need,
And ev'n in Paradise to be a weed.   30

    Ah my deare Father, ease my smart!
These contrarieties crush me: these crosse actions
Doe winde a rope about, and cut my heart:
    And yet since these thy contradictions
Are properly a crosse felt by thy sonne,   35
With but foure words, my words, *Thy will be done.*

The Flower

    How fresh, O Lord, how sweet and clean
Are thy returns! ev'n as the flowers in spring;
    To which, besides their own demean,

The late-past frosts tributes of pleasure bring.
                    Grief melts away   5
                    Like snow in May,
        As if there were no such cold thing.

        Who would have thought my shrivel'd heart
Could have recover'd greennesse? It was gone
                    Quite under ground; as flowers depart   10
To see their mother-root, when they have blown;
                    Where they together
                    All the hard weather,
        Dead to the world, keep house unknown.

        These are thy wonders, Lord of power,   15
Killing and quickning, bringing down to hell
                    And up to heaven in an houre;
Making a chiming of a passing-bell.
                    We say amisse,
                    This or that is: 20
        Thy word is all, if we could spell.

        O that I once past changing were,
Fast in thy Paradise, where no flower can wither!
        Many a spring I shoot up fair,
Offring at heav'n, growing and groning thither: 25
                    Nor doth my flower
                    Want a spring-showre,
        My sinnes and I joining together:

        But while I grow in a straight line,
Still upwards bent, as if heav'n were mine own,   30
        Thy anger comes, and I decline:
What frost to that? what pole is not the zone,
                    Where all things burn,
                    When thou dost turn,
        And the least frown of thine is shown?   35

And now in age I bud again,
After so many deaths I live and write;
I once more smell the dew and rain,
And relish versing: O my onely light,
It cannot be   40
That I am he
On whom thy tempests fell all night.

These are thy wonders, Lord of love,
To make us see we are but flowers that glide:
Which when we once can finde and prove,   45
Thou hast a garden for us, where to bide.
Who would be more,
Swelling through store,
Forfeit their Paradise by their pride.

Dotage

FALSE glozing pleasures, casks of happinesse,
Foolish night-fires, womens and childrens wishes,
Chases in Arras, guilded emptinesse,
Shadows well mounted, dreams in a career,
Embroider'd lyes, nothing between two dishes;   5
These are the pleasures here.

True earnest sorrows, rooted miseries,
Anguish in grain, vexations ripe and blown,
Sure-footed griefs, solid calamities,
Plain demonstrations, evident and cleare,   10
Fetching their proofs ev'n from the very bone;
These are the sorrows here.

But oh the folly of distracted men,
Who griefs in earnest, joyes in jest pursue;
Preferring, like brute beasts, a lothsome den   15
Before a court, ev'n that above so cleare,
Where are no sorrows, but delights more true,
          Then miseries are here!

The Sonne

LET forrain nations of their language boast,
What fine varietie each tongue affords:
I like our language, as our men and coast:
Who cannot dresse it well, want wit, not words.
How neatly doe we give one onely name   5
To parents issue and the sunnes bright starre!
A sonne is light and fruit; a fruitfull flame
Chasing the fathers dimnesse, carri'd farre
From the first man in th' East, to fresh and new
Western discov'ries of posteritie.   10
So in one word our Lords humilitie.
We turn upon him in a sense most true:
   For what Christ once in humblenesse began,
   We him in glorie call, *The Sonne of Man*.

A true Hymne

     MY joy, my life, my crown!
   My heart was meaning all the day,
      Somewhat it fain would say:
And still it runneth mutt'ring up and down
With onely this, *My joy, my life, my crown.*   5

Yet slight not these few words:
If truly said, they may take part
Among the best in art.
The finenesse which a hymne or psalme affords,
Is, when the soul unto the lines accords.   10

He who craves all the minde,
And all the soul, and strength, and time,
If the words onely ryme,
Justly complains, that somewhat is behinde
To make his verse, or write a hymne in kinde.   15

Whereas if th' heart be moved,
Although the verse be somewhat scant,
God doth supplie the want.
As when th' heart sayes (sighing to be approved)
O, could I love! and stops: God writeth, *Loved*.   20

The Answer

My comforts drop and melt away like snow:
I shake my head, and all the thoughts and ends,
Which my fierce youth did bandie, fall and flow
Like leaves about me: or like summer friends,
Flyes of estates and sunne-shine. But to all,   5
Who think me eager, hot, and undertaking,
But in my prosecutions slack and small;
As a young exhalation, newly waking,
Scorns his first bed of dirt, and means the sky;
But cooling by the way, grows pursie and slow,   10
And setling to a cloud, doth live and die
In that dark state of tears: to all, that so
    Show me, and set me, I have one reply,
    Which they that know the rest, know more then I.

The 23d Psalme

THE God of love my shepherd is,
    And he that doth me feed:
While he is mine, and I am his,
    What can I want or need?

He leads me to the tender grasse,   5
    Where I both feed and rest;
Then to the streams that gently passe:
    In both I have the best.

Or if I stray, he doth convert
    And bring my minde in frame: 10
And all this not for my desert,
    But for his holy name.

Yea, in deaths shadie black abode
    Well may I walk, not fear:
For thou art with me; and thy rod   15
    To guide, thy staffe to bear.

Nay, thou dost make me sit and dine,
    Ev'n in my enemies sight:
My head with oyl, my cup with wine
    Runnes over day and night.   20

Surely thy sweet and wondrous love
    Shall measure all my dayes;
And as it never shall remove,
    So neither shall my praise.

Aaron

HOLINESSE on the head,
Light and perfections on the breast,
Harmonious bells below, raising the dead
To leade them unto life and rest.
　　Thus are true Aarons drest. 5

Profanenesse in my head,
Defects and darknesse in my breast,
A noise of passions ringing me for dead
Unto a place where is no rest.
　　Poore priest thus am I drest. 10

Onely another head
I have, another heart and breast,
Another musick, making live not dead,
Without whom I could have no rest:
　　In him I am well drest. 15

Christ is my onely head,
My alone onely heart and breast,
My onely musick, striking me ev'n dead;
That to the old man I may rest,
　　And be in him new drest. 20

So holy in my head,
Perfect and light in my deare breast,
My doctrine tun'd by Christ, (who is not dead,
But lives in me while I do rest)
　　Come people; Aaron's drest. 2.

The Forerunners

THE harbingers are come. See, see their mark;
White is their colour, and behold my head.
But must they have my brain? must they dispark
Those sparkling notions, which therein were bred?
     Must dulnesse turn me to a clod?   5
Yet have they left me, *Thou art still my God.*

Good men ye be, to leave me my best room,
Ev'n all my heart, and what is lodged there:
I passe not, I, what of the rest become,
So *Thou art still my God*, be out of fear.   10
     He will be pleased with that dittie;
And if I please him, I write fine and wittie.

Farewell sweet phrases, lovely metaphors.
But will ye leave me thus? when ye before
Of stews and brothels onely knew the doores,   15
Then did I wash you with my tears, and more,
     Brought you to Church well drest and clad:
My God must have my best, ev'n all I had.

Lovely enchanting language, sugar-cane,
Hony of roses, whither wilt thou flie?   20
Hath some fond lover tic'd thee to thy bane?
And wilt thou leave the Church, and love a stie?
     Fie, thou wilt soil thy broider'd coat,
And hurt thy self, and him that sings the note.

Let foolish lovers, if they will love dung,   25
With canvas, not with arras clothe their shame:

Let follie speak in her own native tongue.
True beautie dwells on high: ours is a flame
      But borrow'd thence to light us thither.
Beautie and beauteous words should go together.   30

Yet if you go, I passe not; take your way:
For, *Thou art still my God*, is all that ye
Perhaps with more embellishment can say.
Go birds of spring: let winter have his fee,
      Let a bleak palenesse chalk the doore,   35
So all within be livelier then before.

The Rose

PRESSE me not to take more pleasure
      In this world of sugred lies,
And to use a larger measure
      Then my strict, yet welcome size.

First, there is no pleasure here: 5
      Colour'd griefs indeed there are,
Blushing woes, that look as cleare
      As if they could beautie spare.

Or if such deceits there be,
      Such delights I meant to say;   10
There are no such things to me,
      Who have pass'd my right away.

But I will not much oppose
      Unto what you now advise:
Onely take this gentle rose,   15
      And therein my answer lies.

104

What is fairer then a rose?
　　　What is sweeter? yet it purgeth.
Purgings enmitie disclose,
　　　Enmitie forbearance urgeth.　　　　　　　20

If then all that worldlings prize
　　　Be contracted to a rose;
Sweetly there indeed it lies,
　　　But it biteth in the close.

So this flower doth judge and sentence　　　　25
　　　Worldly joyes to be a scourge:
For they all produce repentance,
　　　And repentance is a purge.

But I health, not physick choose:
　　　Onely though I you oppose,　　　　　　　30
Say that fairly I refuse,
　　　For my answer is a rose.

The Posie

　　　LET wits contest,
And with their words and posies windows fill:
　　　Lesse then the least
Of all thy mercies, is my posie still.

　　　　This on my ring,　　　　　　　5
This by my picture, in my book I write:
　　　Whether I sing,
Or say, or dictate, this is my delight.

          Invention rest,
Comparisons go play, wit use thy will: 10
          Lesse then the least
Of all Gods mercies, is my posie still.

The Elixir

          TEACH me, my God and King,
            In all things thee to see,
And what I do in any thing,
            To do it as for thee:

          Not rudely, as a beast,   5
            To runne into an action;
But still to make thee prepossest,
            And give it his perfection.

          A man that looks on glasse,
            On it may stay his eye;   10
Or if he pleaseth, through it passe,
            And then the heav'n espie.

          All may of thee partake:
            Nothing can be so mean,
Which with his tincture (for thy sake)   15
            Will not grow bright and clean.

          A servant with this clause
            Makes drudgerie divine:
Who sweeps a room, as for thy laws,
            Makes that and th' action fine.   20

This is the famous stone
That turneth all to gold:
For that which God doth touch and own
Cannot for lesse be told.

A Wreath

A WREATHED garland of deserved praise,
Of praise deserved, unto thee I give,
I give to thee, who knowest all my wayes,
My crooked winding wayes, wherein I live,
Wherein I die, not live: for life is straight,   5
Straight as a line, and ever tends to thee,
To thee, who art more farre above deceit,
Then deceit seems above simplicitie.
Give me simplicitie, that I may live,
So live and like, that I may know thy wayes,   10
Know them and practise them: then shall I give
For this poore wreath, give thee a crown of praise.

Love (III)

LOVE bade me welcome: yet my soul drew back,
    Guiltie of dust and sinne.
But quick-ey'd Love, observing me grow slack
    From my first entrance in,
Drew nearer to me, sweetly questioning,   5
    If I lack'd any thing.

A guest, I answer'd, worthy to be here:
        Love said, you shall be he.
I the unkinde, ungratefull? Ah my deare,
        I cannot look on thee.   10
Love took my hand, and smiling did reply,
        Who made the eyes but I?

Truth Lord, but I have marr'd them: let my shame
        Go where it doth deserve.
And know you not, sayes Love, who bore the blame?   15
        My deare, then I will serve.
You must sit down, sayes Love, and taste my meat:
        So I did sit and eat.

Sonnets *from* Walton's Lives

My God, where is that ancient heat towards thee,
    Wherewith whole showls of *Martyrs* once did burn,
    Besides their other flames. Doth Poetry
Wear *Venus* Livery? only serve her turn?
Why are not *Sonnets* made of thee? and layes   5
    Upon thine Altar burnt? Cannot thy love
    Heighten a spirit to sound out thy praise
As well as any she? Cannot thy *Dove*
Out-strip their *Cupid* easily in flight?
    Or, since thy wayes are deep, and still the same,   10
    Will not a verse run smooth that bears thy name!
Why doth that fire which by thy power and might
    Each breast does feel, no braver fuel choose
    Than that, which one day, Worms, may chance refuse.

Sᴜʀᴇ Lord, there is enough in thee to dry   15
    Oceans of *Ink*; for, as the Deluge did
    Cover the Earth, so doth thy Majesty:
Each Cloud distills thy praise, and doth forbid
Poets to turn it to another use.
    Roses and *Lillies* speak thee; and to make   20
    A pair of Cheeks of them, is thy abuse.
Why should I *Womens eyes* for Chrystal take?
Such poor invention burns in their low mind
    Whose fire is wild, and doth not upward go
    To praise, and on thee Lord, some *Ink* bestow.   25
Open the bones, and you shall nothing find
    In the best *face* but *filth*, when Lord, in thee
    The *beauty* lies, in the *discovery*.

Extracts from

A PRIEST TO THE TEMPLE

OR,

THE COUNTREY PARSON

HIS CHARACTER

AND RULE OF HOLY LIFE

Chapter 4

The Parsons Knowledg

THE Countrey Parson is full of all knowledg. They say, it is an ill
Mason that refuseth any stone: and there is no knowledg, but, in a
skilfull hand, serves either positively as it is, or else to illustrate some
other knowledge. He condescends even to the knowledge of tillage,
and pastorage, and makes great use of them in teaching, because
people by what they understand, are best led to what they under-
stand not. But the chief and top of his knowledge consists in the
book of books, the storehouse and magazene of life and comfort,
the holy Scriptures. There he sucks, and lives. In the Scriptures hee
findes four things; Precepts for life, Doctrines for knowledge,
Examples for illustration, and Promises for comfort: These he hath
digested severally. . . .

Chapter 7

The Parson preaching

. . . When he preacheth, he procures attention by all possible art, both by earnestnesse of speech, it being naturall to men to think, that where is much earnestness, there is somewhat worth hearing; and by a diligent, and busy cast of his eye on his auditors, with letting them know, that he observes who marks, and who not; and with particularizing of his speech now to the younger sort, then to the elder, now to the poor, and now to the rich. This is for you, and This is for you; for particulars ever touch, and awake more then generalls. Herein also he serves himselfe of the judgements of God, as of those of antient times, so especially of the late ones; and those most, which are nearest to his Parish; for people are very attentive at such discourses, and think it behoves them to be so, when God is so neer them, and even over their heads. Sometimes he tells them, stories, and sayings of others, according as his text invites him; for them also men heed, and remember better then exhortations; which though earnest, yet often dy with the Sermon, especially with Countrey people; which are thick, and heavy, and hard to raise to a poynt of Zeal, and fervency, and need a mountaine of fire to kindle them; but stories and sayings they will remember. He often tels them, that Sermons are dangerous things, that none goes out of Church as he came in, but either better, or worse; that none is careless before his Judg, and that the word of God shal judge us. By these and other means the Parson procures attention; but the character of his Sermon is Holiness; he is not witty, or learned, or eloquent, but Holy. A Character, that *Hermogenes* never dream'd of, and therefore he could give no precept thereof. But it is gained first, by choosing texts of Devotion, not Controversie, moving and ravishing texts, whereof the Scriptures are full. Secondly, by dipping, and seasoning all our words and sentences in our hearts, before they come into our mouths, truly affecting, and cordially expressing all that we say; so that the auditors may plainly perceive that every word is hart-deep. Thirdly, by turning often, and making many Apostrophes to God, as, Oh Lord blesse my people, and teach them this point; or, Oh my Master, on whose errand I come, let me hold my peace, and doe thou speak thy selfe; for thou art Love, and when thou teachest, all are Scholers. . . .

Chapter 10

The Parson in his house

. . . The furniture of his house is very plain, but clean, whole, and sweet, as sweet as his garden can make; for he hath no mony for such things, charity being his only perfume, which deserves cost when he can spare it. His fare is plain, and common, but wholsome, what hee hath, is little, but very good; it consisteth most of mutton, beefe, and veal, if he addes any thing for a great day, or a stranger, his garden or orchard supplyes it, or his barne, and back-side: he goes no further for any entertainment, lest he goe into the world, esteeming it absurd, that he should exceed, who teacheth others temperance. But those which his home produceth, he refuseth not, as coming cheap, and easie, and arising from the improvement of things, which otherwise would be lost. Wherein he admires and imitates the wonderfull providence and thrift of the great house-holder of the world: for there being two things, which as they are, are unuseful to man, the one for smalnesse, as crums, and scattered corn, and the like; the other for the foulnesse, as wash, and durt, and things thereinto fallen; God hath provided Creatures for both; for the first, Poultry; for the second, swine. These save man the labour, and doing that which either he could not do, or was not fit for him to do, by taking both sorts of food into them, do as it were dresse and prepare both for man in themselves, by growing them selves fit for his table. . . .

Chapter 13

The Parson's Church

THE Countrey Parson hath a speciall care of his Church, that all things there be decent, and befitting his Name by which it is called. Therefore first he takes order, that all things be in good repair; as walls plaistered, windows glazed, floore paved, seats whole, firm, and uniform, especially that the Pulpit, and Desk, and Communion Table, and Font be as they ought, for those great duties that are performed in them. Secondly, that the Church be swept, and kept cleane without dust, or Cobwebs, and at great festivalls strawed, and stuck with boughs, and perfumed with incense. Thirdly, That there be fit, and proper texts of Scripture every where painted, and that all the painting be grave, and reverend, not with light colours, or foolish anticks. Fourthly, That all the books appointed by Authority be there, and those not torne, or fouled, but whole and clean, and well bound; and that there be a fitting, and sightly Communion Cloth *of fine linnen, with an handsome, and seemly Carpet of good and costly Stuffe, or Cloth, and all kept sweet and clean, in a strong and decent chest, with a Chalice, and Cover, and a Stoop, or Flagon; and a Bason for Almes and offerings; besides which, he hath a Poor-mans Box conveniently seated, to receive the charity of well minded people, and to lay up treasure for the sick and needy*. And all this he doth, not as out of necessity, or as putting a holiness in the things, but as desiring to keep the middle way between superstition, and slovenlinesse, and as following the Apostles two great and admirable

Rules in things of this nature: The first whereof is, *Let all things be done decently, and in order*: The second, *Let all things be done to edification*, 1 *Cor*. 14. For these two rules comprize and include the double object of our duty, God, and our neighbour; the first being for the honour of God; the second for the benefit of our neighbor. So that they excellently score out the way, and fully, and exactly contain, even in externall and indifferent things, what course is to be taken; and put them to great shame, who deny the Scripture to be perfect.

Chapter 14

The Parson in Circuit

. . . WHEN he comes to any house, first he blesseth it, and then as hee finds the persons of the house imployed, so he formes his discourse. Those that he findes religiously imployed, hee both commends them much, and furthers them when hee is gone, in their imployment; as if hee findes them reading, hee furnisheth them with good books; if curing poor people, hee supplies them with Receipts, and instructs them further in that skill, shewing them how acceptable such works are to God, and wishing them ever to do the Cures with their own hands, and not to put them over to servants. Those that he finds busie in the works of their calling, he commendeth them also: for it is a good and just thing for every one to do their own busines. But then he admonisheth them of two things; first, that they dive not too deep into worldly affairs, plunging themselves over head and eares into carking, and caring; but that they so labour, as neither to labour anxiously, nor distrustfully, nor profanely. Then they labour anxiously, when they overdo it, to the loss of their quiet, and health: then distrustfully, when they doubt Gods providence, thinking that their own labour is the cause of their thriving as if it were in their own hands to thrive, or not to thrive. *Then they labour profanely, when they set themselves to work like brute beasts, never raising their thoughts to God, nor sanctifying their labour with daily prayer; when on the Lords day they do unnecessary servile work, or in time of divine service on other holy days, except in the cases of extreme poverty, and in the seasons of Seed-time, and Harvest.* Secondly, he adviseth them so to labour for wealth and maintenance, as that they make not that the end of their labour, but that they may have wherewithall to serve God the better, and to do good deeds. . . .

. . . he holds the Rule, that Nothing is little in Gods service: If it once have the honour of that Name, it grows great instantly. Wherfore neither disdaineth he to enter into the poorest Cottage, though he even creep into it, and though it smell never so lothsomly. For both God is there also, and those for whom God dyed: and so much the rather doth he so, as his accesse to the poor is more comfortable, then to the rich; and in regard of himselfe, it is more humiliation. . . .

Chapter 21

The Parson Catechizing

. . . When once all have learned the words of the Catechisme, he thinks it the most usefull way that a Pastor can take, to go over the same, but in other words: for many say the Catechisme by rote, as parrats, without ever piercing into the sense of it. In this course the order of the Catechisme would be kept, but the rest varyed: as thus, in the Creed: How came this world to be as it is? Was it made, or came it by chance? Who made it? Did you see God make it? Then are there some things to be beleeved that are not seen? Is this the nature of beliefe? Is not Christianity full of such things, as are not to be seen, but beleeved? You said, God made the world;

Who is God? And so forward, requiring answers to all these, and helping and cherishing the Answerer, by making the Question very plaine with comparisons, and making much even of a word of truth from him. This order being used to one, would be a little varyed to another. And this is an admirable way of teaching, wherein the Catechized will at length finde delight, and by which the Catechizer, if he once get the skill of it, will draw out of ignorant and silly souls, even the dark and deep points of Religion. *Socrates* did thus in Philosophy, who held that the seeds of all truths lay in every body, and accordingly by questions well ordered he found Philosophy in silly Trades-men. That position will not hold in Christianity, because it contains things above nature: but after that the Catechisme is once learn'd, that which nature is towards Philosophy, the Catechism is towards Divinity. To this purpose, some dialogues in *Plato* were worth the reading, where the singular dexterity of *Socrates* in this kind may be observed, and imitated. Yet the skill consists but in these three points: First, an aim and mark of the whole discourse, whither to drive the Answerer, which the Questionist must have in his mind before any question be propounded, upon which and to which the questions are to be chained. Secondly, a most plain and easie framing the question, even containing in vertue the answer also, especially to the more ignorant. Thirdly, when the answer sticks, an illustrating the thing by something else, which he knows, making what hee knows to serve him in that which he knows not: As, when the Parson once demanded after other questions about mans misery; since man is so miserable, what is to be done? And the answerer could not tell; He asked him again, what he would do, if he were in a ditch? This familiar illustration made the answer so plaine, that he was even ashamed of his ignorance; for he could not but say, he would hast out of it as fast as he could. Then he proceeded to ask, whether he could get out of the ditch alone, or whether he needed a helper, and who was that helper. This is the skill, and doubtlesse the Holy Scripture intends thus much, when it condescends to the naming of a plough, a hatchet, a bushell, leaven, boyes piping and dancing;

shewing that things of ordinary use are not only to serve in the
way of drudgery, but to be washed, and cleansed, and serve for
lights even of Heavenly Truths. . . .

Chapter 23

The Parson's Completenesse

. . . And let *Fernelius* be the Phisick Authour, for he writes briefly,
neatly, and judiciously; especially let his Method of Phisick be
diligently perused, as being the practicall part, and of most use.
Now both the reading of him, and the knowing of herbs may be
done at such times, as they may be a help, and a recreation to more
divine studies, Nature serving Grace both in comfort of diversion,
and the benefit of application when need requires; as also by way
of illustration, even as our Saviour made plants and seeds to teach
the people: for he was the true householder, who bringeth out of
his treasure things new and old; the old things of Philosophy, and
the new of Grace; and maketh the one serve the other. And I con-
ceive, our Saviour did this for three reasons: first, that by familiar
things hee might make his Doctrine slip the more easily into the
hearts even of the meanest. Secondly, that labouring people (whom
he chiefly considered) might have every where monuments of his
Doctrine, remembring in gardens, his mustard-seed, and lillyes; in
the field, his seed-corn, and tares; and so not be drowned altogether
in the works of their vocation, but sometimes lift up their minds
to better things, even in the midst of their pains. Thirdly, that he
might set a Copy for Parsons. In the knowledge of simples, wherein
the manifold wisedome of God is wonderfully to be seen, one thing
would be carefully observed; which is, to know what herbs may
be used in stead of drugs of the same nature, and to make the garden
the shop: For home-bred medicines are both more easie for the

Parsons purse, and more familiar for all mens bodyes. So, where the Apothecary useth either for loosing, Rubarb, or for binding Bolearmena, the Parson useth damask or white Roses for the one and plantaine, shepherds purse, knot-grasse for the other, and that with better successe. As for spices, he doth not onely prefer home-bred things before them, but condemns them for vanities, and so shuts them out of his family, esteeming that there is no spice comparable, for herbs, to rosemary, time, savoury, mints; and for seeds, to Fennell, and Carroway seeds. Accordingly, for salves, his wife seeks not the city, but preferrs her garden and fields before all outlandish gums. And surely hyssope, valerian, mercury, adder tongue, yerrow, melilot, and Saint *Johns* wort made into a salve And Elder, camomill, mallowes, comphrey and smallage made into a Poultis, have done great and rare cures. . . .

Chapter 33

The Parson's Library

THE Countrey Parson's Library is a holy Life: for besides the blessing that that brings upon it, there being a promise, that if the Kingdome of God be first sought, all other things shall be added even it selfe is a Sermon. For the temptations with which a good man is beset, and the ways which he used to overcome them, being told to another, whether in private conference, or in the Church are a Sermon. Hee that hath considered how to carry himself at table about his appetite, if he tells this to another, preacheth; and much more feelingly, and judiciously, then he writes his rules of temperance out of bookes. So that the Parson having studied, and mastered all his lusts and affections within, and the whole Army of Temptations without, hath ever so many sermons ready penn'd as he hath victories. . . .

COMMENTARY AND NOTES

3. THE ALTAR

There were many precedents for the shaped poem, both classical and contemporary. Herbert very probably knew the examples of wing and altar patterns in 'The Greek Anthology'; Puttenham's *Arte of English Poesie* (1589) has a whole chapter, entitled 'Of Proportion in figure', devoted to shaped poems; and the dedicatory verses of Sylvester's *Du Bartas His Devine Veekes and Workes* (1605-8) are patterned.

3-4. The idea behind these lines relates to Deut. 27.5: 'And there shalt thou build an altar unto the Lord thy God, an altar of stones: thou shalt not lift up any iron tool upon them.' See also Exod. 20.25.

6. Zech. 7.12: 'Yea, they made their hearts as an adamant stone, lest they should hear the law . . . therefore came a great wrath from the Lord of hosts.'

13-14. Luke 19.40: 'I tell you that, if these should hold their peace, the stones would immediately cry out.'

3. THE SACRIFICE

The Sacrifice covers the events of Holy Week. In tone and method it is unlike any other poem by Herbert; it takes the form of a dramatic monologue spoken by Christ, and is made up of a series of antitheses which reflect the paradoxical nature of Christianity. Its grandeur derives from the poet's ability to transmute into poetry the great paradox that the Man who had to suffer is indeed God (see lines 69-73).

God's compassion and God's justice—these two are subtly juxtaposed in tone that blends pity with irony. In lines 149-52, for instance, together with Christ's compassionate advice to his 'deare friends' not to weep for him 'since I for both have wept', is an implication of impending justice: their tears will be needed for themselves since they abandoned him in his agony—'Your tears for your own fortunes should be kept'. This blend of compassion and irony recurs frequently throughout the poem, and only by careful scrutiny of each antithesis and its various implications can the full force of *The Sacrifice* be appreciated. Notice particularly how each recurrence of the refrain, 'Was ever grief like mine', has a slightly different, and often ambiguous, implication.

As Rosemond Tuve (*A Reading of George Herbert*) has shown, the creation of a monologue for the suffering Christ, and many of the ironies and paradoxes themselves, are not Herbert's invention, for the whole style is embedded in Christian liturgy and medieval poetry. Herbert, however, has made the style completely his own, exploring and developing paradoxes implicit in the tradition.

William Empson has a study of the poem in *Seven Types of Ambiguity* (Chap. 7).

*l.*1. *all ye, who passe by:* This quotation is from 1.12 and 2.15 of the Lamentations of Jeremiah, where the City of Jerusalem speaks a monologue. See also Mat. 27.39: 'And they that passed by reviled him, wagging their heads.'

*ll.*5–6. *The Princes . . . their Maker:* See Psalm 2.2 (*B.C.P.*).

*l.*7. See Exod. 16.1–16.

*l.*10. See Deut. 5.15.

*l.*11. In John 19.11 this paradox is expressed in Jesus' words to Pilate: 'Thou couldest have no power at all against me, except it were given thee from above.'

*l.*13. See John 12.6.

*l.*18. See John 12.5.

*l.*22. See Luke 22.44.

*l.*23. The whole line is in apposition to 'my words'. See Luke 22.42.

*l.*37. Mat. 26.55: 'Are ye come out as against a thief with swords and staves for to take me?'

*l.*38. *way & Truth:* This is the reading of both MSS. 1633 reads 'way of truth'. See John 14.6.

*ll.*45–6. *See, they lay hold . . . but furie:* 1.Tim. 6.12: 'Fight the good fight of faith, lay hold on eternal life.'

*l.*47. Ezek. 34.27: They 'shall know that I am the Lord, when I have broken the bands of their yoke.'

*l.*55. *Comments would the text confound:* 'My explanations of their law would destroy its meaning.'

*l.*57. *The Priest:* i.e. Caiaphas the high Priest, who upheld the false witnesses. See Mat. 26.57–66.

*l.*59. See Isa. 53.7, Jer. 11.19, and Acts 8.32.

*l.*62.   See John 10.33.

*l.*63.   This paradox appears in Phil. 2.6: 'Who, being in the form of God, thought it not robbery to be equal with God.'

*ll.*65–6.   See John 2.19–21.

*ll.*69–71.   The great paradox here is that man sins with the breath that Christ gives him.

   Thus Adam . . . rendereth: This is how man returns God's gift of the breath of life (Gen. 2.7).

*l.*74.   *This makes them agree:* See Luke 23.12.

*l.*77.   *set me light:* make light of me; despise and deride me.

*l.*78.   Psalm 144.1 (*B.C.P.*): 'Blessed be the Lord my strength: who teacheth my hands to war, and my fingers to fight.'

*l.*79.   *Hosts:* B. and W. 'hosts' 1633.

*l.*85.   *despitefulnesse:* contemptuousness; derision.

*l.*86.   *vying:* here used transitively; matching.

*l.*107.   Mat. 27.25: 'Then answered all the people, and said, His blood be on us, and on our children.'

*l.*109.   *These words:* i.e. the 'wish' of *l.*107.

*l.*115.   'it' (i.e. murder, *l.*113) was naturally approved by those who killed me.

*l.*119.   *more then heav'n doth glasse:* 'more than heaven surpasses glass (in transparency etc.).'

*l.*121.   *Caesar:* B. 'Cesar' W. and 1633. John 19.15: 'Pilate saith unto them, Shall I crucify your King? The chief priests answered, We have no king but Caesar.'

*ll.*122–3.   Num. 20.11: 'And Moses lifted up his hand, and with his rod he smote the rock twice: and the water came out abundantly;' in Psalm 78.21 (B.C.P.) it was God who 'smote the stony rock indeed, that the water gushed out'. Thus Moses is traditionally identified with the deity. The 'He' of *l.*122, however, seems to refer to 'Caesar' of the previous line; in which case the reference to cleaving the rock in *l.*122 is heavily ironic: 'What, do you really think that *he*, Caesar, gave you the life-giving water? —*he* cannot soften your hearts, as I know by experience.' Caesar has been mistaken for the true king, Christ.

*l.*126.   *Doubles:* 'because I feel pain so easily, because I feel it painful that they should be so cruel, because I feel it painful they should be so unjust, because my tenderness enrages them, because my tenderness (being in fact power) will return equally each stroke upon them, because I take upon myself those pains also.' (Empson)

ll.126-7.   *their bitterness . . . mysteriousness:* i.e. their bitterness adds to my grief the mystery of love repaid by hate.

l.129.   The sudden change to the third personal pronoun in both MSS obviously worried the 1633 editor, who alters to the first person. However in the present reading from B. and W. Christ can still remain the speaker without any sense of discontinuity, and perhaps, as Hutchinson suggests, Herbert is 'heightening the insolence of the soldiers in maltreating one who is the ruler of the universe'.

l.130.   *grasps:* B. 'graspes' W. 'grasp' 1633.

l.134.   See John 9.6.

l.137.   See Luke 22.64.

l.138.   Exod. 34.33-4: 'And till Moses had done speaking with them [the children of Israel], he put a vail on his face. But when Moses went in before the Lord to speak with him, he took the vail off.' See also 2 Cor. 12-16.

l.139.   *either:* the Law of the Old Testament, represented by Moses; and the Gospels, the New Dispensation given by Christ.

l.141.   *abjects:* 'One cast off; an outcast; a degraded person' (*O.E.D.*, citing this example). See Psalm 35.15 (*B.C.P.*).

l.146.   *calls:* B. and W. 'cals' 1633. *utmost breath:* an ambiguity implying, 'shouting their utmost, strenuous shouting', and 'last, dying, breath'.

l.149.   See Luke 23.28.

l.150.   See Luke 22.44.

l.155.   See Mat 26.53.

ll.161-3.   The thorns of the Crucifixion are here related to the vine of Sion, the house of Israel; though God has planted and watered the vine, this crown of thorns is all it bears. The thorns, grapes and vine of the vineyard of the house of Israel occur together in Isa. 5.1-7.

l.165.   The reference is to the curse of thorns in Gen. 3.18: 'Thorns also and thistles shall it bring forth to thee.'

l.170.   In 1 Cor. 10.4 Christ as a rock is identified with the rock which Moses struck (see *l*.122): the children of Israel 'did all drink the same spiritual drink: for they drank of that spiritual Rock that followed them: and that Rock was Christ.'

l.174.   &: B. and W. 'or' 1633.

l.178.   *weeds:* clothing.

l.183.   See Luke 10.24.

l.185.   *trimmed:* arrayed, dressed.

l.193.   *ingrosse:* form of 'engross', concentrate.

l.201.   At the start of the climax to the poem the quotation from Lamentations (see *l*.1 and note) is extended—Lam. 1.12: 'Is it nothing to you, all ye that pass by? behold, and see if there be any sorrow like unto my sorrow.'

ll.201–3.   The parallel of the tree of Paradise with the tree of the Cross was a convention in medieval literature and liturgy. Tuve quotes: 'Who hast established the salvation of mankind by the wood of the cross, that so whence death arose, from thence life might arise again, and that he who by a tree had gained a victory might by a tree be also overcome.' (Preface to the feasts of the Holy Cross, *Sarum Missal*, translated by Frederick E. Warren.)

   but onely me: except me alone.

ll.205–7.   *th' two:* the world of sin and the natural world; the world of sin is the greater since it can only be redeemed by sorrow, whereas the natural world came into being simply by divine command.

l.218.   'Sharp nails pierce my body; but sharper nails confound my soul,' namely, the reproaches of the next stanza.

l.221.   See Luke 4.23, and Mat. 27.40 and 42.

l.231.   *Death:* B. and W. 'death' 1633.

l.233.   See Mat. 27.37.

l.237.   *give:* B. and W. 'gave' 1633.

l.239.   Psalm 78.26 (*B.C.P.*): 'So man did eat angels' food: for he sent them meat enough.'

l.242.   *which once cur'd:* Mat. 14.36: the sick were brought to Jesus 'that they might only touch the hem of his garment: and as many as touched were made perfectly whole'.

l.247.   As Eve came from Adam's side, so 'blood and water', signifying the sacraments, flowed from Christ's side, pierced at the Crucifixion. See John 19.34.

ll.251–2.   Empson points to a possible double meaning here: 'After the death of Christ, may there never be a grief like Christ's;' and, 'Only let there *be* a retribution, only let my torturers say never was grief like theirs, in the day when my agony shall be exceeded.'

Herbert tries to offer an equivalent for each of God's gifts. In lines 1–10 he follows the events of the Passion, and in each instance concludes that he cannot emulate God. So he will imitate His love, and enumerates the possible ways of doing so (*ll.*17–28). Interrupted by the thought of the Passion (*ll.*29–30), he continues his list of good works, declares he will love God as much as God loves him, and ends by claiming the victory (*ll.*47–8). Again, however, the thought of the Passion brings Herbert to submission.

*l.*4. *preventest:* 'to anticipate in action' (*O.E.D.*); this leads to the idea: 'To outdo, surpass, excel' (*O.E.D.*). There is also the implication that, by its very nature, God's experience of grief hinders Herbert's grief. See Psalm 21.3 (*B.C.P.*).

*ll.*5–6. See Luke 22.44 and also *The Sacrifice l.*150.

doore: This word has been found difficult, as can be seen from the emendation to 'gore' in most editions after 1678. 'It is an outlet for the blood; cf. Shakespeare, *Julius Caesar* III.ii.182–4' (Hutchinson). Herbert is also enlarging upon the Biblical idea of Christ as the door to Heaven. See John 10.9 and Introduction p. 17.

*ll.*9–10. 'Your words on the Cross expressed a grief which I cannot hope to emulate.' The whole of line 9 is the subject of 'was' in line 10. See Mat. 27.46, and *The Sacrifice l.*213.

*l.*11. *skipping:* ignoring, passing over, or (as appears in W.) neglecting. 1633 is punctuated 'skipping, thy dolefull storie'. B. does not have this comma.

*l.*13. *strokes be my stroking:* 'The play on words would have been more readily apprehended in Herbert's day because of such current spelling as is found in the A.V., e.g. John XVIII.22: "one of the officers which stood by, stroke Iesus with the palme of his hand".' (Hutchinson)

*l.*14. *Thy rod, my posie?* This might be a reference to 'Aaron's rod that budded' (Heb. 9.4).

Posie: 'A bunch of flowers; a nosegay, a bouquet' (*O.E.D.*). Herbert could be making a pun on posy as 'a short motto' (*O.E.D.*). The word is also used 'sometimes in the sense of Poesy, a poetical reproduction' (*O.E.D.*). i.e. 'will the rod that struck you result in poetry (this poem) by me?' See *ll.*39–47, where a further reference is made to his own poetry.

*l.*17. *revenge:* B. and W. *'reuenge'* 1633.

revenge me on thy love: rival your love.

*l.*19. *wealth,* B. 'wealth;' W. and 1633.

l.20.   *by:* by means of. See Proverbs 19.17.

l.21.   *honour,* B. 'honour;' W. and 1633.

ll.25–6.   *thence:* refers to the position of the friend as 'bosome friend'. 'If my bosom friend blasphemes your name, I shall tear his love from me, and the high regard which I have for him, from my breast.'

ll.27–8.   These lines are difficult. Palmer makes 'one half of me' the 'bosome friend'. 'The rest' seems to refer not only to himself (i.e. he will dedicate himself to the service of the Church), but also to his worldly wealth; for he writes that he will donate 'the rest' whether he lives or dies.

l.30.   *the other:* i.e. the other points of your doctrine and life.

ll.31–2.   'The *predestination* may refer to the ministry of Jesus, those three years in which he was about his Father's business.' (Palmer)

ll.33–4.   *spittle:* hospital, more especially for the poor; alms-house.

The pun on *wayes* ('roads', 'habits') is a good example of Herbert's quiet humour.

ll.35–6.   'I shall only have anything to do with worldly things for appearance's sake.'

ll.37–8.   'I shall become so detached from temporal things that no-one will notice that I am still alive.'

l.40.   *his attribute:* its own particular quality. The reference is to the lute, which in Herbert's time had anything between sixteen and thirty strings.

l.44.   *'tis here:* i.e. in my book of poems, as opposed to 'thy book' (the Bible) of line 45.

l.47.   *Thy art of love:* as opposed to the *Ars Amatoria* of Ovid. *thee* with colon: W. 'thee,' B. and 1633.

ll.48–50.   When Herbert cries 'Victorie!' he imagines he has turned God's love back on Him, in accordance with his determination in line 17 to 'revenge me on thy love'. Herbert thinks he has won the contest 'who shall victorious prove' (*l*.18), until he remembers Christ's Passion, which had already eluded him in lines 29–30.

44.   THE REPRISALL

This poem, which in *The Temple* immediately follows *The Thanksgiving*, is a direct extension of the thought in the first poem. The beginning of *The Reprisall* sums up the situation at the end of *The Thanksgiving*; Herbert goes on to demonstrate the impossibility of emulating God, and concludes that he must not fight against Him (as he had tried in *The Thanksgiving*), but become part of God's conquest by conquering himself.

Title: The connection with the previous poem is made more obvious in W. by the title *The Second Thanksgiving.* The significance of 'reprisal' is less obvious. Palmer suggests a wide definition which would include the general notion of Herbert's trying to please God: 'A Reprisal is an attempt to return in kind what has been received whether of good or ill.' Its more particular relevance would be to lines 15–16, where Herbert implies that he will make reprisals on himself, and overcome his previous rebellious spirit towards God.

*ll.*3–4. 'Even if I died for you (as you died for mankind), I am too late, for my sins have already made me fit for condemnation.'

*ll.*5–6. 'Make me innocent, so that I may be disentangled from sin, and therefore free (to give you my life).'

*ll.*7–8. 'And yet (even if I were innocent) by your wounds you would always defy my attempts to give you my life freely, for it is only through the strength given me by your death that I could die for you.' Herbert is saying that he cannot die for God in the same way as God died for him, since he will always be indebted to God.

*ll.*13–14. *will I come/Into thy conquest:* i.e. I will be part of your victory. He has already made one false attempt in *The Thanksgiving* (*l.*48).

thy conquest with colon: B. 'thy conquest,' W. 'the conquest.' 1633.

*l.*15. *in thee:* through you, with your help.

*l.*16. *The man:* i.e. myself, who once fought against you; the human part of me which wants to rebel against you; the old Adam.

45. THE AGONIE

This poem is a fine example of Herbert using Christian thought in an original and subtle manner to elucidate important aspects of human experience. The wine-press, a traditional Biblical type for judgement and dispensation (e.g. the Fall of Babylon, Rev. 4.19–20), is here an image for the Passion and Crucifixion. By means of it Herbert throws light on the essential connection between good and evil. Through an understanding of his own sinfulness (the wine-press) man will be able to find, to experience ('assay and taste'), goodness; just so for the Christian the experiencing of the truth of the Crucifixion, in itself an example of man's sinfulness, will lead to salvation.

*l.*1. *Philosophers:* In Herbert's time the word had a wider application, denoting men learned in physical science, as well as in the metaphysical and moral sciences.

l.3.   *staffe:* 'a rod for measuring distances and heights' (*O.E.D.*). Scientists have measured the distance between the earth and heavenly bodies. Herbert also implies the traveller's staff; hence the notion of walking with it to heaven. Both kinds are otherwise known as Jacob's staff (Gen. 32.10). See *Divinitie l.*27.

   traced fountains: i.e. traced the course of a spring to its source; this carries on the ideas of travelling and measuring.

*l.*8.   *mount Olivet:* this stanza refers to the Agony in the Garden on the Mount of Olives (Luke 22.39).

*l.*9.   *wrung:* foreshadows the wine-press metaphor of *l.*11.

*l.*10.   See Luke 22.44 and *The Thanksgiving l.*5.

*l.*11.   *presse:* Isa. 63.3: 'I have trodden the winepress alone; . . . for I will tread them in mine anger, and trample them in my fury; and their blood shall be sprinkled upon my garments, and I will stain all my raiment.'

   vice: the pun emphasizes the tight hold 'sinne' has upon man.

*l.*12.   *his:* its.

stanza 3: From the Agony in the Garden Herbert extends the metaphor to the wine-press of the Crucifixion.

*l.*14.   *that juice:* the wine/blood of the eucharist.

*ll.*14–15.   *which on the crosse . . . abroach:* After Jesus' death on the Cross, 'one of the soldiers with a spear pierced his side, and forthwith came there out blood and water' (John 19.34). The crucified Christ is seen as a barrel of wine broached for man to drink.

*ll.*17–18.   'a kind of inversion of the doctrine of transubstantiation; the blood of the Divine Sufferer is to the man who receives it "as wine" that refreshes and revives, and the meaning of the gift is love.' (Hutchinson: 'George Herbert' in *Seventeenth Century Studies presented to Sir Herbert Grierson.*) The idea of Christ's blood as reviving drink is expressed in John 6.55. See *Divinitie l.*21.

45. REDEMPTION

   This poem is an allegorical account of the granting of the Covenant of Grace. The old lease is the Covenant of Works, by which mankind, the tenant, was obliged to give the profits of the land to God, his landlord. The 'new small-rented lease' is the Covenant of Grace, by which God, in sending his own Son, made possible man's Redemption.

   This poem appears in W. as *The Passion.* See Introduction, p. 18.

l.3. Herbert's suit probably has its Biblical counterpart in the thief's request at the Crucifixion for a place in God's kingdom (Luke 23.42).

l.8. *Long since:* long ago.

l.14. *Your suit is granted:* Jesus replies to the thief: 'Verily I say unto thee, To day shalt thou be with me in paradise.' (Luke 23.43)

46. EASTER

stanza 1: The general thought is from Romans 6 and Colossians 2.12: Jesus having died for our sins, we died to sin in His death; when He rose from the dead, we rose with Him into 'newness of life'.

l.3. *thee:* i.e. the heart.

ll.5–6. *calcined:* The more general sense is 'to burn to ashes, consume' (*O.E.D.*, citing this example). But Herbert is also using the word with its alchemical reference: the alchemists believed that, by burning off its impure substances, they could reduce a mineral to its purest form (in *l.*5 Herbert jokes on the word 'dust'), out of which gold could be formed. Just so, Christ's death burns the sinful and impure substances from man's heart, which is then brought by His Resurrection to a new life, free from impurities.

l.6. *and much more, just:* Herbert's sudden humour aptly readjusts the reference to death to suit the happy tone of a poem dedicated to 'this most high day'. He may be thinking of the proverb, 'as good as gold'; or the tendency of gold as money to become unjust.

more, W. 'more' no comma B. and 1633.

l.7. See the Easter Psalm, 57.9 (*B.C.P.*): 'awake, lute and harp: I myself will awake right early.'

l.9. See *The Temper (I)*, *ll.* 22–24, where lute and rack are juxtaposed.

ll.11–12. *stretched:* B. and W. 'streched' 1633. *what key . . . high day:* 'the choice of keys was significant because the doctrine of affections coordinated certain keys with certain affections.' (Quoted by J. H. Summers from Manfred F. Bukofzer, *Music in the Baroque Era*.)

l.13. *twist a song:* 'Figuratively, from the plaiting of fibres into a cord; cf. Shakespeare, *Much Ado*, I.i.321: "to twist so fine a story". It is especially appropriate to polyphonic music.' (Hutchinson)

ll.15–17. *vied:* 'To increase in number by addition or repetition' (*O.E.D.*, citing this example). The song of heart and lute would be incomplete without the Spirit's part to make up the common triad. See Rom. 8.26: 'the Spirit also helpeth our infirmities.'

multiplied: perhaps refers to the repetition of such chords. 'multiplied' no punctuation B. and W. 'multiplied;' 1633.

*l.*19.   This is the 'song' proposed in *l.*13.

See Christ's entry into Jerusalem, Mat. 21.8: 'others cut down branches from the trees, and strawed them in the way.'

*ll.*24–6.   'Though the sun gives light and the East gives perfume,they would be presumptuous to compare their gifts with those ("thy sweets", *l.*22) of *Easter.*'

*l.*29.   *three hundred:* the number of days in a year in round numbers.

*l.*30.   'There is only one important sun: the one which rises on Easter day —and that shines for eternity.'

47.   EASTER-WINGS

For the tradition of shaped poems, see introductory note to *The Altar*, p. 119. For discussion see Introduction, p. 28.

This text follows B. and W. in printing the lines of the poem horizontally. 1633 prints vertically.

*l.*8.   *larks:* the central image of the poem.

*l.*10.   'The paradox that Adam's sin (*felix culpa*) occasioned the glorious Redemption is familiar in St. Augustine and in medieval writers' (Hutchinson). See also Rom. 5.20.

*l.*19.   *imp:* in falconry, 'To engraft feathers in the wing of a bird, so as to make good losses or deficiencies, and thus restore or improve the powers of flight.' (*O.E.D.*)

48.   NATURE

*l.*2.   *travell:* 'his Mother would by no means allow him to leave the University, or to travel.' (Walton, *Lives.*)

*l.*6.   See 2 Cor. 10.4.

*l.*7.   *this venome:* i.e. the 'rebellion' of *l.*1.

*l.*9.   *bubbles:* i.e. high flying rebellious thoughts.

*l.*10.   *by kinde:* according to the nature of bubbles. See *A true Hymn l.*15.

*ll.*13–14.   Jer. 31.33: 'I will put my law in their inward parts, and write it in their hearts.' See also *Vanitie* (*I*) *ll.*23–4.

*ll.*15–18.   Ezek. 36.26: 'A new heart also will I give you, and a new spirit will I put within you: and I will take away the stony heart out of your flesh, and I will give you a heart of flesh.' For a more elaborate treatment of the heart/stone metaphor see *The Altar.*

49. SINNE (I)

A sonnet in the Shakespearean pattern. Herbert lists three types of protection: in the first quatrain, that of our elders; in the second, that of religion; and in the third, that of social awareness.

Coleridge wrote of this poem: 'equally admirable for the weight, number and expression of the thoughts, and for the simple dignity of the language (unless indeed a fastidious taste should object to the latter half of the sixth line).' (*Biographia Literaria*, Chap. 19.)

*l.*3.   *they:* i.e. the schoolmasters.

*l.*6.   *sorted:* every variety of.

*l.*11.   *shame:* i.e. disgrace.

49. AFFLICTION (I)

This poem is one of Herbert's finest demonstrations that religious faith expressed in poetry need be no limitation to the poet's emotional response. Because of its fidelity to emotional detail *Affliction (I)* is a remarkable personal record of inner conflict. The poet is perhaps interested not so much in resolving the conflict, as in recognizing it, and through it himself. This is achieved through subtle ambiguity of tone and meaning, and with a paradoxical conclusion which brings together and heightens the elements of conflict—rebellion and acquiescence. It is the honesty with which Herbert conveys the pain of self-recognition which makes the poem a powerful human record.

The reader is referred to two admirable studies: in L. C. Knights, 'George Herbert', essay in *Explorations*; and in William Empson, *Seven Types of Ambiguity*, Chap. 6.

*ll.*3–6.   i.e. in the holy life Herbert saw pleasures which he thought would make a free addition to those he already possessed.

*ll.*11–12.   *starres:* here represent a glorious payment. In his poem *The Church-porch* Herbert writes:

> Take starres for money; starres not to be told
> By any art, yet to be purchased.   (*ll.*171–2)

*l.*13.   'I lacked no pleasures when I served pleasure's king.'

*l.*18.   *youth and fierceness:* The implication is that youth and fierceness are not qualities of the soul which would be ready to serve; this prepares us for the disillusionment at the end of the next stanza.

*l.*24.   *made a partie:* raised a faction.

*l.*25.   *began:* 'Either a misprint, or a noticeable idiom of the word "began"?

Yes! and a very beautiful idiom it is;—the first colloquy or address of the flesh.' (Coleridge: notes on *The Temple*.) 'The flesh in pain at last begins to remonstrate with the idealizing soul, and utters its complaint in the following three lines, in which, it will be noticed, all the verbs are in the present tense.' (Hutchinson)

l.35. fence: defence.

l.40. Refers to the scholar's life.

ll.43–4. for I threatned . . . mine age: 'Because I often threatened to relinquish my attempts at an academic and clerical life, being unable to find preferment among men of the time . . .'. In his Church calling the ambitious side of Herbert's nature was having no outlet.

simpring: probably a reference to the feigning smile needed to curry favour with people of influence. 'Simpring is but a lay-hypocrisie' (*The Church-porch, l.*123).

l.45. Thus keeping him to university life and eventual priesthood.

ll.47–8. where: W. The reading of B. is 'neere,' underlined, and 'where' written above. 'neare;' 1633.

till I came where . . . persevere: 'Till I came to a point or a state of mind from which I could neither bring myself to withdraw nor to continue in my present course whole-heartedly.' (Hutchinson)

l.53. crosse-bias me: 'give me an inclination other than my own' (Grierson, *Metaphysical Lyrics and Poems*). The verb 'to bias' is a metaphor from the game of bowls.

ll.61–6. In the final stanza Herbert's mood vacillates rapidly between resignation and rebellion. Finally, with the affirmation of his allegiance to the love of God, this conflict culminates in a paradoxical statement which is both a rebellious protest at the pain of loving God, and an acceptance of His love in its entirety:

though I am clean . . . love thee not: 'Even if it means I shall be completely forgotten by you, let me be released from the pains of loving you if I cannot love you entirely.'

52. PRAYER (I)

This sonnet takes the form of a definition by a rapid succession of analogies, a technique popular among Elizabethan sonneteers, especially Sidney (e.g. his sonnets 79 and 80 in *Astrophel and Stella*). Notice that the metaphors are expressed without the use of a single connective verb. T. S. Eliot called the effect of the final phrase 'magical'.

Angels age: This could mean that prayer is as old as the angels; or '*Angels age* is contrasted with "Mans age" . . . prayer acquaints man with the blessed timeless existence of the angels.' (Hutchinson)

l.2. The breath which God gave man is returned to Him in the form of prayer.

l.3. *The soul in paraphrase:* i.e. prayer helps the soul to express itself more clearly and fully.

l.5. *Engine against th'Almightie:* In his poem *Artillerie* Herbert regards prayer as arrows to be shot at God.

l.7. *six-daies world:* In Genesis the creation took six days.

transposing: here means 'altering' or 'transforming'.

l.10. *Exalted Manna:* Instead of falling from Heaven this manna rises up to it.

l.11. *in ordinarie:* in common life.

52. ANTIPHON (I)

Antiphon: 'A composition, in prose or verse, consisting of verses or passages sung alternately by two choirs in worship.' (*O.E.D.*)

l.12. 'The reference is to part-singing in choir or madrigal consort. The certain meaning is "chief, or most important part"—but "fundamental part" would bring out the musical implication well. For probably the suggestion behind *longest* is of the most active part-line, containing the major proportion of sustained notes, a foundation for the harmony.' (Douglas Brown, *Selected Poems of George Herbert*.)

53. LOVE I AND II

It is probable that these two sonnets are a complete re-write of the two early sonnets sent by Herbert to his mother (p. 108). The theme and much of the imagery are the same; but whereas the early poems consist of a series of fervent hyperboles (reminiscent of Donne's forceful style), in the later the materials are worked into an argument, and the strident tone has disappeared.

The later sonnets make two complementary patterns skilfully matched. In the first Herbert complains that love has been turned from God, and in the second prays that it may be directed towards Him. The symmetry of the argument is reflected in vocabulary, structure and imagery—for instance, the parallel phrasing of the first lines; the use of 'ame' and 'ain' rhymes in both poems; the connection of 'wit' with 'beautie' in the first sonnet, and in the second, because of a twist in the argument, of 'wit' with 'dust'; the use of the words 'invention', 'heart' and 'brain' in both poems.

For discussion see Introduction, p. 18.

LOVE I

l.4.   on that dust which thou hast made: i.e. on human beings, created out of dust (Gen. 2.7).

l.5.   the title: i.e. the title of love.

l.6.   invention: 'Almost a technical term in rhetoric: e.g. Obadiah Walker, *Oratory* (1659), p. 1: "The Parts of Oratory are Invention, taking care for the Matter; and Elocution, for the Words and Style". ' (Hutchinson.) Invention is the matter which the imagination finds for the embodying of the poet's abstract conception.

LOVE II

l.6.   pant thee: pant for thee; or perhaps 'pant towards thee', implying breathlessness. See Psalm 42.1.

ll.11–12.   recover, disseized: both legal terms.

recover: 'to obtain, by legal process, possession or restoration of the thing claimed.' (*O.E.D.*)

disseize: 'to dispossess (a person) of his estates, etc., usually wrongfully or by force.' (*O.E.D.*)

The inference is that Love possesses the world by right.

*l.14.   See *Love (III) l.12.

54.   THE TEMPER (1)

Distress at the inconstancy of his feelings towards God is a recurring theme with Herbert—see for instance *The Glimpse.* Here, the poem is itself a demonstration of his fluctuating spirits. The various suggestions presented in the treatment of images reflect each change in mood, until, in the final stanza, a state of equilibrium is reached. Notice the delightfully witty tone. *Title:* Even though the word is never used in the poem, 'temper' is its unifying concept. The references to 'steel' and 'music' (see notes below) recall the title, as does of course the general subject-matter, Herbert's temperament. (Formerly 'temper' could have the same significance as does 'temperament' today—one's habitual disposition.) The poem's conclusion points to a more particular significance: 'mental balance or composure, . . . moderation in or command over the emotions; calmness, equanimity'

(*O.E.D.*). Today we use the word thus only in phrases such as 'to lose one's temper'. In W. the poem is entitled *The Christian Temper*.

ll.1–3. The gist is, 'how much I would praise you, God, if only I could always feel towards you what I occasionally feel'.

l.2. engrave thy love in steel: steel is hardened, or 'tempered', and the engraving would thus be a lasting tribute to God.

stanza 2: Herbert goes on to illustrate the variableness of his feelings.

l.5. fourtie: often used in the Bible (especially the Old Testament) to signify 'many'.

l.9. Herbert implores God not to stretch him on the huge rack which goes between the heaven and hell of the previous stanza.

l.10. i.e. those distances (between heaven and hell) are *your* province, or 'befit thy nature' (Hutchinson); but do not extend *me* that far.

ll.11–12. for, although the world is too small to be *your* habitation, for *me* it is . . .

1 Kings 8.27: 'But will God indeed dwell on earth? behold, the heaven and heaven of heavens cannot contain thee; how much less this house that I have builded?'

tent: probably used with Biblical overtones of the Tabernacle and the Ark of the Covenant: 'the tabernacle, namely, the tent of the testimony.' (Num. 9.15. See also Exod. 40.19; 2 Sam. 7.6; 1 Chr. 17.5.)

ll.13–14. 'Are you so anxious to contend with man, that you will make him your equal (in combat) by stretching him, a mere crumb of dust?' 'There is a play on the word *mete* (cf. *measure l.15*), as of those who measure arms before fighting a duel.' (Hutchinson)

l.16. spell: 'To consider, contemplate, scan intently.' (*O.E.D.*)

stanza 5: Whereas the previous stanzas are about God's 'stretching' of Herbert, this asks that he may be contracted.

ll.17–20. If 'roof' means Heaven, Herbert is asking to be given a secure resting-place there, with the implication (*ll.19–20*) that he would be away from the temptations of the world. However, perhaps 'roof' recalls 'tent' (*l.11*), in which case the emphasis is slightly different; 'roof' could then mean God's tabernacle (see notes to *ll.11–12*), His Church, with the gist: 'make me content to rest in your Church, and I shall then no longer be a sinner (since I shall not be subject to these fluctuations of the spirit)'.

l.22. me, 'mee,' B. and W. 'me' no comma 1633.

ll.23–4. The merging of images here is elliptical. The stretching and contracting of the rack suggests the stretching and contracting of the sinews of his heart, a lute whose strings are thus tuned so as to make better music to God. This is another implied reference to 'temper': 'to tune, adjust the pitch of (a musical instrument)' (*O.E.D.*). i.e. Herbert's fluctuations of mood are God's way of testing his love, and of making him more able to sing God's praises. In the final stanza Herbert does just this, and the object of *l.*1 ('How should I praise thee') is achieved.

*l.*26.   *there:* i.e. in a place made by you.

*l.*28.   since all places are pervaded by the presence of God.

55. JORDAN (I)

For discussion of this poem and *Jordan (II)* see Introduction, p. 18.

Title: Various explanations have been made, and probably more than one significance is intended. The river Jordan represents baptismal cleansing, the consecration of Herbert's poetry to Christianity rather than to the pagan muse associated with Helicon. There is probably an allusion to 2 Kings 5.10, where Elisha counsels Naaman to wash in Jordan rather than in the rivers of Damascus: 'Go and wash in Jordan seven times, and thy flesh shall come again to thee, and thou shalt be clean.' And crossing the Jordan into the Promised Land is a traditional symbol of conversion.

*l.*5.   'The chair or throne of grace filled by God is true compared with the painted chairs of the love-poets.' (Palmer)

*l.*6.   *except:* unless.

*l.*7.   *sudden arbours:* 'that appear unexpectedly, it being an aim of the designer of a garden that it should have surprises.' (Hutchinson)

shadow: The arbours cast a shadow upon the lines, thus masking the deficiencies of the verse (i.e. the subject of the poem is more important than its workmanship); or, the arbours cast a shadow and make the lines difficult to perceive and understand (i.e. the paraphernalia of pastoral imagery obscures the meaning of the lines).

course-spunne lines: irregular and difficult lines of poetry, like thread which has been badly spun.

*l.*8.   *purling:* flowing with a whirling motion and bubbling sound.

*l.*11.   *Shepherds:* i.e. the shepherds who wrote in eclogue, lyric, elegy, pastoral, etc.

*l.*12.   *Riddle who list, for me:* 'let anyone make up riddles who wants to, so far as I am concerned, . . .'

pull for Prime: i.e. strive to be best; in the card-game of Primero, 'to

135

draw for a card or cards which will make the player "prime".' (*O.E.D.*, citing this example.)

l.15. *plainly say:* compare 'sing' of *l*.11.

My God, My King: See *Antiphon* (*I*) and *The Elixir l*.1.

56. EMPLOYMENT (I)

Whereas here Herbert sees himself dependent on God for employment, he creates a slightly different emphasis in *Employment* (*II*) by laying the blame for inactivity on mankind.

ll.1–4. See *The Flower* for an elaboration of this metaphor.

l.2. *extend:* unfold, give opportunity for enlargement. So also in *l*.6.

ll.5–8. The gist is: 'the praise would go to you for enlarging me; but I too would then be found worthy of occupying a place in your order of creation ("thy garland" of flowers, "thy great chain" of *l*.21) when the Day of Judgment ("thy great doom") comes.'

ll.11–12. 'Only on earth is joy measured quantitively; and you are the one who possesses its substance'—implying: please give me some.

l.16. i.e. even though life is slow in coming to its end.

ll.17–20.   *that:* i.e. the honey
these: i.e. the flowers.

In this stanza Herbert creates a 'chain'—water, flowers, bee, honey—in which, he says, he has no part.

l.21. *thy great chain:* The idea of the chain of being began with Plato's *Timaeus*, and was developed by Aristotle; it was spread by the Neo-Platonists, and from the Middle Ages became an accepted commonplace. The concept of the chain underlay much Elizabethan thought and literature, and survived into the eighteenth century (Pope: 'Vast chain of Being', *Essay on Man*, I.237). The chain linked the highest order of creation, the angels, down through all ranks of existence, to the smallest inanimate objects. Milton has the concept in mind in *Paradise Lost*, V.469 ff., and it underlies the thought of Herbert's poem *Man*. The reader should study Ulysses' speech on Order in Shakespeare's *Troilus and Cressida*, I.iii.85–137, for the full implications of the doctrine.

l.22. 'I am as useless to society as a weed.' i.e. he is not the 'flowre' of *l*.1 and *l*.19. See *The Crosse, l*.30.

l.23. *consort*=concert: 'A company or set of musicians, vocal or instrumental, making music together' (*O.E.D.*). Order is part of the divine harmony; see *Troilus and Cressida* I.iii.109–10:

Take but degree away, untune that string,
And hark what discord follows.

57. CHURCH-MONUMENTS

This poem is remarkable for the sustained movement of the lines; the lack of end-stopping, the building up of loosely connected clauses, the steady pace of the verse unimpeded by pauses, make *Church-monuments* perhaps more reminiscent of Donne's style than any other poem by Herbert. 'Dust' with its rhyme-words 'trust', 'lust', and its assonants 'blast', 'last'; the string of open vowels, 'laugh', 'bow', 'wanton', 'crumbled', etc.; the unostentatious rhymes; all make this a perfectly cadenced poem on the theme of death.

Recognizing the six-line rhyme scheme, 1633 prints in three stanzas. However, this text follows both MSS. in setting the poem out unbroken, thus reinforcing the uninterrupted flow of the verse.

*ll.*8–9. The body 'comprehends' what elements it is composed of by regarding the tomb. There is possibly a pun on 'spell'; for also the inscription (the 'heraldrie and lines') would be 'spelt out' because it is 'dustie' and therefore difficult to decipher.

*ll.*10–11. The 'heraldrie and lines' give the ancestry of the onlooker, showing how all shall turn to dust. There is also possibly the suggestion that the 'heraldrie and lines' make an ironical comparison between the dust on the tomb and the dust into which the ancestors have dissolved.

*l.*12. *These:* i.e. dust and earth.

Jeat: 1633 second ed. 'leat' 1633 first ed.

*ll.*17–24. The flesh has a lesson to learn from the monument. Just as the monument holds the dust of dead bodies, so our flesh, like an hour-glass, holds the dust of our lives (the deeds by which our days are measured). The containers—monument, flesh, hour-glass—will crumble into a dust indistinguishable from the dust that they contain. By recognizing this fact the flesh will lose its pride and 'lust', and thus be prepared for the eventual dissolution.

58. THE CHURCH-FLOORE

The symbolism, which seems at first abstract and arbitrary, the difficulty in understanding what Herbert is comparing the church floor to, gives this poem an ambiguous and slightly puzzling tone. It is not until the final couplet gently surprises the reader that each detail becomes clear and alive:

it is the marble heart that weeps, and Death, instead of sullying the heart by reminding us of the flesh's frailty ('the dust'), purifies and strengthens it by blowing away our imperfections. For the idea of the heart as the temple of God see Acts 7.48: 'Howbeit the most High dwelleth not in temples made with hands'; and 1 Cor. 3.16: 'Know ye not that ye are the temple of God, and that the Spirit of God dwelleth in you?'

l.10.   Col. 3.14: 'And above all these things put on charity, which is the bond of perfectness.'

l.14.   *neat*: In the seventeenth century the precise sense of this word is not always clear. The most likely connotations here are: clean, free from impurities; clear, bright.

   curious: 'Made with care or art; skilfully, elaborately or beautifully wrought.' (*O.E.D.*)

ll.16–18.   See *Church-monuments* for a different treatment of the death/dust theme.

59.   THE WINDOWS

Of the group of poems about the priesthood *Aaron* was almost undoubtedly written when Herbert was already a priest, and *The Priesthood* just before he became one. This poem, however, contains less obviously personal references, although Herbert's concern with the priest's way of life and its effect on the congregation would seem to indicate that *The Windows* was written some time during the Bemerton period.

As in *Man* and *The Church-floore* man is God's temple; the preacher is both window and glass through which the 'eternall word' can reach the people. If, however, he leads a good life, having the story of Christ 'annealed' in him, the preacher will be more effective, colourful like the stained-glass window, not 'watrish, bleak, and thin'.

l.6.   *anneal*: 'To burn in colours upon glass, earthenware, or metal.' (*O.E.D.*)

59.   CONTENT

Notice the gentle humour and aphoristic style with which Herbert here treats the subject of ambition. Although maxims are scattered throughout his work, only one other poem, *The Church-porch* (not in this selection), is as markedly aphoristic as this. Herbert was very probably the collector and translator of a considerable part of *Outlandish Proverbs*, a book of foreign proverbs.

l.5.   *quest:* a metaphor from hunting. 'The baying of hounds in pursuit of game.' (*O.E.D.*, citing this example.)

l.8.   i.e. excessive watchfulness.

l.15.   *let loose to:* technical phrase in archery: aim at, as one lets an arrow loose at a target. Probably Herbert intends a pun, with the secondary meaning 'let go of'.

l.16.   *Take up:* proceed to occupy. The reference is probably to the Emperor Charles V, who in 1556 abdicated his throne and retired to a cloister; it was a stock example, and is mentioned by both Walton and Oley in their Lives of Herbert.

l.18.   *From either pole:* i.e. between both poles.

l.21.   *brags:* 'Show, pomp, display; pompous demeanour or carriage.' (*O.E.D.*, citing this example.)

l.25.   *Onely thy Chronicle is lost:* 'The only difference between you and famous men is that there will be no record of your life remaining.' Donne, *The Canonization*, ll.31–2:

> And if no peece of Chronicle wee prove,
> We'll build in sonnets pretty roomes.

l.27.   *fret:* 'To gnaw; to consume, torture or wear away by gnawing' (*O.E.D.*). Psalm 39.12 (*B.C.P.*): 'like as it were a moth fretting a garment'.

l.28.   *rent:* a variant of 'rend', tear. The verb is intransitive here. The idea is that human bodies will not last as long as books.

l.29.   *deeds, whose brunt thou feel'st alone:* 'Only you can know the effort needed to accomplish your deeds.'

ll.31–2.   *digestion* is in apposition to 'wit', and continues the metaphor begun by 'chaw'd' and 'tongue'. 'The state of posterity's intellectual appetite will determine the reputation to which you gave so much care.'

l.33.   *discoursing:* used in the early sense of 'passing rapidly from one thought to another; busily thinking.' (*O.E.D.*)

l.36.   *ever:* W. 'euer' B. and 1633.

61. THE QUIDDITIE

Title: Quiddity, originally a scholastic term for 'the real nature or essence of a thing' (*O.E.D.*), came to mean 'a subtlety or captious nicety in argument, a quirk, quibble' (*O.E.D.*). In W. the poem is entitled simply *Poetry*.

l.10.   *Hall:* 'probably the hall of a Livery Company, in which business was transacted for the sale of the members' goods.' (Hutchinson)

l.12.   *and Most take all:* perhaps, 'and it is then (when I am writing poetry and with you) that I most exert myself.' Herbert's poetry is the 'quiddity' or essence of all his actions. F. P. Wilson (*A Note on George Herbert's 'The Quidditie'* in *Review of English Studies*, Vol. 19, 1943), pointing to the fact that 'most take all' is a worldly proverb (with the gist 'the most powerful take everything'), concludes that Herbert has characteristically changed it to express his surrender to God. He paraphrases: 'God the all-powerful takes complete possession of him [the poet].'

61. EMPLOYMENT (II)

l.2. would: wishes to.

l.4. furre: warm clothing needed by the inactive; and academic dress: 'those budge doctors of the Stoic Fur.' (Milton, *Comus, l.*707.)

l.5. cold complexions: In medieval theory a person's 'complexion' was composed of the four 'humours' or bodily fluids, their proportions determining his natural disposition. Each humour of the microcosm, or little world of man, had its counterpart in the four elements of which the universe is composed. Thus, choler corresponded to fire, and was hot and dry; blood corresponded to air (hot and moist); phlegm corresponded to water (cold and moist); black bile corresponded to earth (cold and dry). So a cold complexion would be one in which black bile, or earth (*l.*14), predominated.

l.6. a quick coal: 'A piece of carbon glowing without flame' (*O.E.D.*), in contrast to dead coal, as in *Vertue, l.*15.

*ll.*11–15. *th 'elements:* see notes to *l.*5. Fire was supposed to be the highest (*l.*13) of the elements, and earth (*l.*14) the lowest because the most inert. Thus there is a danger that he who is inactive (see stanza 2) will find a similarly low place.

*l.*18. The sun is always shining somewhere. Herbert is saying that we should be in action perpetually, like the sun, rather than occasionally, like the stars, which can only appear when the sun is absent.

*ll.*21–2. The Orange is busy because it bears blossom and fruit both at the same time. Herbert is particularly fond of the tree metaphor; see *Man, l.*8; *Affliction (I), l.*57; *Affliction (V), l.*20.

*ll.*26–8. We make excuses that we are either too young or too old to begin anything, until the Man (who 'dressed me') has gone (i.e. life has slipped by) and we have missed the opportunity to produce any goods for him.

*l.*27. *Man:* B. and W. 'man' 1633.

62. DENIALL

In this poem spiritual anxiety, disappointed hopes, and a feeling of use-lessness, are poignantly conveyed. 'Then was my heart broken, as was my verse' is the key to the poem; throughout the 'broken' quality of the verse —for instance the rhythmical dropping away of the last line in each stanza, the absence of the final rhyme—we feel the pull of the regular beat and rhyme which Herbert denies us. Until, with its prayer for help, the last stanza establishes the underlying pattern, and harmony is restored with the words 'mend my ryme'.

Notice how the music imagery reinforces this concern for harmony. In line 6 his thoughts are like a 'brittle bow', his soul is an 'untun'd, unstrung' lute in lines 21–2, and in the final stanza Herbert asks that his 'heartlesse breast' may be tuned.

l.22.   *Untun'd, unstrung:* see note to *Employment (I)*, *l.23*, p. 136.

l.26.   *tune my heartlesse breast:* see *The Temper (I)*, *l.23*, and note.

64. VANITIE (I)

l.2.   *the spheres:* In Ptolemaic astronomy nine concentric hollow crystal spheres surround the earth, and carry the heavenly bodies through their orbits.

l.3.   See *The Agonie*, *l.3*.

l.5.   *their dances:* The stars were supposed to be in continual dance. In Sir John Davies' poem *Orchestra, or a Poem of Dancing* the universe is seen as a dance:

> The turning vault of heaven formed was,
> Whose starry wheels he hath so made to pass,
> As that their movings do a music frame,
> And they themselves still dance unto the same.   (*ll.*130–4)

and in *Much Ado* (2.1.314) Beatrice says: 'there was a star danced, and under that was I born'.

l.6.   i.e. he can forecast the position of any star.

l.7.   *aspects:* in astronomy, 'aspect' is the angular distance between two planets as seen from the earth's surface at any given moment; in astrology this was supposed to influence earthly matters. Literally the term means the way in which the planets look at one another, and hence the reference to 'full ey'd' aspects and to 'secret glances'.

ll.15–21.   'The chemist in his laboratory is, as it were, *admitted to* the *bedchamber* of the object of his inquiry, and he can there unclothe it (*devest*) and *strip* it of the feathers which disguise it (cf. *callow*, featherless), so as to discover its interior *principles*; he can give his mind to their study (*l.*18) with better opportunity than those can who only see them emerge from *the doore* fully drest.' (Hutchinson)

*ll.*23–4. Jer. 31.33: 'I will put my law in their inward parts, and write it in their hearts.'

*ll.*27–8. If man acknowledges the law which is at hand, within himself, he will receive salvation ('life'); man's 'vanity', his pride, is in ignoring salvation in his search for knowledge (which is thus 'death').

65. VERTUE

In the first three stanzas the day, the rose, and the spring are shown to come to a natural end. The virtuous soul, on the other hand, in a metaphor which contrasts it with the mortality of the world, is shown to be everlasting.

*l.*2. The day marks the wedding of earth and sky.

*l.*3. *thy fall:* the short last line of each stanza is itself a 'dying fall'.

*l.*5. *angrie:* 'Having the colour of an angry face, red.' (*O.E.D.*, citing this example.)

*l.*10. *sweets:* perfumes.

*l.*11. *closes:* a 'close' is the technical name for a cadence or conclusion of a musical phrase.

*ll.*15–16. 'Even though (in the final conflagration) the whole world turns to cinder, ashes ("coal": *O.E.D.* 2b), virtue will survive and remain glowing.'

65. THE PEARL

Alongside the poem's title Herbert gives a reference to Mat. 13.45: 'Again, the kingdom of heaven is like unto a merchant man, seeking goodly pearls: Who, when he had found one pearl of great price, went and sold all that he had, and bought it.' The poem relates what Herbert sold in order to buy the pearl.

The poem's conclusion acknowledges that his efforts will only succeed if they are coupled with God's guidance and grace. In the first three stanzas we see this dual process at work: the many knowledgeable references to learning, honour and pleasure, and the witty style of a man of the world, show how great had to be Herbert's effort to forego a way of life which so allured him. In contrast, the simple statement of devotion in the short line at the end of each stanza—'Yet I love thee'—demonstrates the guidance and grace of God at work in the poet.

ll.1–2. It is probable that the printing-press was suggested to Herbert by a wine or olive press, and that there is an allusion to Zechariah's vision of the seven lamps—Zech. 4.12: 'two olive branches which through the two golden pipes empty the golden oil out of themselves' (to feed the bowl for the lamps). 'Perhaps *the head* is the fountain of knowledge, the universities, and the *pipes* are those who mediate that knowledge to the world in the learned professions.' (Hutchinson)

l.6. 'what nature reveals of her own accord, and what she is forced to reveal by the alchemist's fire.'

l.8. *stock and surplus:* perhaps inherited knowledge, and the knowledge we have added to it.

ll.11–12. *what maintains . . . and wit:* a trading metaphor: 'what continues the quick profits of courtesy and wit.'

ll.13–17. 'I can tell which party gains the upper hand in a contest of doing favours; when ambition swells the heart, and makes the heart compliant to any deed or look which will win the world, and which will carry the bundle of favours thus gained wherever the world goes.'

ll.21–4. Herbert describes pleasure in musical terms:

strains: the more precise reference is to a definite section of a piece of music, a portion of a movement. In a wider sense 'strain' means a melody or tune.

lullings: gentle refrains, soothing songs.

relishes: ornaments or embellishments used in the performance of music for lute, viol and keyboard.

propositions: a form of *proposta*, the leading part of a fugue (answered by the *riposta*).

l.26. *projects of unbridled store:* schemes of ungoverned wealth.

l.29. i.e. the single will has to curb five senses.

l.31. *in my hand:* at my disposal.

l.32. *sealed:* B. and 1633 spell like this; W. spells 'seeled'. 'Seel' is a term in falconry for sewing up a hawk's eyelids, and perhaps Herbert is making specific reference to this meaning.

ll.33–40. 'I fully understand the terms of sale, and the benefits involved ("commodities", *O.E.D.*), and the price I must pay for your love, with all the conditions that may persuade me; however, it is not my wisdom but your guidance which has prompted my efforts to reach you.'

l.37.   *these:* B. and W. 'the' 1633.

l.38.   *silk twist:* cord composed of silk fibres wound round one another.

67.   AFFLICTION (IV)

l.3.   Psalm 31.12 (A.V.): 'I am forgotten as a dead man out of mind.'

l.4.   Psalm 71.7 (A.V.): I am as a wonder unto many; but thou art my strong refuge.'

ll.7–12.   'Herbert uses a metaphor (watering-pots) within a metaphor (knives) and then gets back to knives (*l*.12), the word *scatter'd* being common to the description of the effects of the knives and of the watering-pots.' (Hutchinson.) Notice the use of 'scatter' again in *l*.23.

   pink: 'To pierce, prick, or stab with any pointed weapon or instrument' (*O.E.D.*). pink B. and W. 'prick' 1633.

l.13.   *attendants:* i.e. the physical functions of the body.

l.15.   'before my very face.'

l.17.   *elements:* see note to *l*.5 of *Employment* (*II*), p. 140.

l.18.   *trie out their right:* the elements contend to see which is superior.

l.30.   *more*, B. and W. 'more' no comma 1633.

68.   MAN

The thought of this poem depends upon the chain of being (see note to line 21 of *Employment* (*I*), p. 136) and the correspondences between the microcosm, the little world of man, and the macrocosm of the universe. The theory, continued into Herbert's day by Bacon and others, held that man, being the meeting place of the lower and higher orders of the chain, contained all the faculties, spiritual and bestial, of the universe.

In this beautifully worked out argument Herbert begins with the proposition that no one builds a 'stately habitation' unless he means to dwell in it. Through the next stanzas he gives the reasons for claiming that man himself is this habitation, and finally implores God to fulfil the purpose of building it by coming to dwell in mankind.

l.2.   This casual allusion in the first line of the poem to a day occurs also in *Affliction* (*V*)—'My God, I read this day'—and the same technique is used by Vaughan: 'I saw Eternity the other night' (*The World*), and 'I walkt the other day (to spend my hour).'

ll.5–6.   *to whose creation . . . decay:* Perhaps means that animals, vegetables, fruits, etc. are destroyed in order to sustain man; or that all things compared with man are underdeveloped (this making a better link with the following stanzas).

ll.7–8. *For Man is ev'ry thing, And more:* man is a microcosm, but he is also more than that; and in the rest of the stanza Herbert explains why this should be so.

l.8. *more fruit:* B. and 1633 have 'no fruit'. I follow the reading of W., as does Hutchinson, who argues that the sense of the whole passage seems to demand 'more'. Man is better than trees because he bears more abundance, greater variety, of fruit.

ll.10–11. The emphasis is on 'we' and 'us': 'Only we (in contrast to the beasts) possess reason and speech; if any other animals speak, e.g. the parrot, they owe it to us.'

l.12. i.e. are in man's debt, 'score' being an account for goods obtained on credit (*O.E.D.*).

l.18. In the theory of microcosm and macrocosm the different parts of the body are affected by the movements of the moon, stars and planets.

l.21. *dismount:* bring down to earth.

ll.25–6. Herbert is referring to the four elements.

ll.34–6. The chain of being underlies the thought of these lines. 'All things in positions below us (on the chain of being) are natural, akin ('kinde') to our flesh; all things in positions above us (on that chain) stretching towards the First Great Cause, are akin to our mind.

l.39. *Distinguished:* Coleridge (notes on *The Temple*) wrote: 'I understand this but imperfectly. Distinguished—they form an island?' But see Gen. 1.9–10: when God 'united' (*l.*38) the waters, gathering them together into seas, they were 'distinguished', i.e. separated, from the land, which then became man's 'habitation'.

l.40. *Below:* i.e. in springs.
    above, our meat: rain is needed for fruit to grow.

l.41. *Hath one such beautie?* 'If a single element, water, has such a variety of good uses, may we not expect the other elements to have a similar aptness for man's service?' (Hutchinson)

l.42. *neat:* cleverly made (compare *The Church-floore*, *l.*14, and see note).

l.45. *that which doth befriend him:* i.e. herbs and flowers, which were supposed to be of medicinal value.

70. LIFE

Like *Vertue*, this poem shows Herbert's characteristically reconciled attitude towards death.

ll.1–3. *Posie* is a nosegay or bouquet, and *ll.*2–3 are what Herbert said to himself when he made the posy. But 'posie' can also mean a motto, a verse, poetry (see note to *l*.14 of *The Thanksgiving*, p. 124), and *ll*.2–3 would then be the lines of poesy which Herbert made 'while the day ran by'.

l.12. *suspicion*: apprehension.

l.15. 'So, where the Apothecary useth either for loosing, Rubarb, or for binding, Bolearmena, the Parson useth damask or white Roses for the one, and plantaine, shepherds purse, knot-grasse for the other, and that with better successe.' *The Country Parson*, Chap. 23. See also *The Rose*, *l*.18.

70. AFFLICTION (V)

The central image of this poem, 'thy floting Ark' (*l*.3), refers to the traditional Christian parallel of the Church with Noah's ark. See the Baptismal Office: 'that he, being delivered from thy wrath, may be received into the ark of Christ's Church; and being stedfast in faith, joyful through hope, and rooted in charity, may so pass the waves of this troublesome world, that finally he may come to the land of everlasting life.' It is worth comparing this poem with *Affliction* (*I*), where the cross-currents of affliction demonstrate what Herbert affirms in this poem—that 'We are the trees, whom shaking fastens more' (*l*.20).

l.2. *planted Paradise*: Gen. 2.8: 'And the Lord God planted a garden eastward in Eden.'

ll.7–10. Compare stanzas 3 and 4 of *Affliction* (*I*).

l.9. *wanton*: 'Undisciplined, ungoverned; not amenable to control, unmanageable, rebellious.' (*O.E.D.*)

ll.11–12. i.e. as we at first shared your joy, so now you share our misery.

ll.15–17. These lines could either mean, 'Joy is for the angels; but if *our* deliverance requires that we experience grief, then at least you offer us baits of both joy and grief'; or, 'Angels have brought us joy; so that if our deliverance requires grief, at least you offer us (by means of the angels) a double bait.'

l.21. *bowres*: 'A place closed in or overarched with branches of trees.' (*O.E.D.*)

l.22. *curious* see note to *l*.14 of *The Church-floore*.

knots: 'A flower-bed laid out in a fanciful or intricate design' (*O.E.D.*). Shakespeare, *Love's Labour's Lost*, I.i.240: 'thy curious-knotted garden'.

store: abundance.

l.24. The rainbow continues the metaphor of the ark (*l*.3). After the Flood God said: 'I do set my bow in the cloud, and it shall be for a token of a covenant between me and the earth' (Gen. 9.13). But 'bow' also suggests the instrument of divine punishment. (See for example Isa. 41.2.)

71. MORTIFICATION

The subject of this poem is the presence of death in life. The needs of death, a shroud, a grave, a bell, a coffin and a bier, are foreshadowed in the needs of man's five ages. The linking of death with the life-giving breath of Genesis in the repeated breath/death rhyme emphasizes the great disparity and similarity about which the whole poem turns. Herbert ends with the prayer that this realization of the presence of death in life may enable him to find 'life in death'.

l.2.   sweets: As in *Easter l.22* and *Vertue l.10* 'sweets' are sweet odours, perfumes.

l.4.   Borrowed from the first line of Donne's *A Funeral Elegy:* 'Sorrow, who to this house scarce knew the way.'

l.5.   clouts: pieces of cloth, often used to signify swaddling clothes.

l.12.   Convey: 'implies not only "to bear to the final destination", but also has the overtone of enslavement, "to carry away secretly".' (J. H. Summers, *George Herbert, His Religion & Art.*)

bound for death: The principal metaphor is of a passenger on board ship being carried over the 'rolling waves' (*l.11*) towards death. But, as J. H. Summers points out, 'bound' also implies the chains in which passengers are forcibly shackled (see 'bindes', *l.9*).

ll.17–18.   knell: the passing-bell, which in Herbert's day was rung while someone was dying, not, as later, only after death. As Hutchinson points out, this makes the reading of W., 'houre of death' (*l.18*) more likely than that of B. and 1633, 'house of death'.

l.24.   attends: is in store for, awaits.

l.26.   Marking: observing; perhaps also, outlining.

l.29.   A chair or litter: 'The use of the word *chair* has more point when it is remembered that in Herbert's day it was a symbol of old age.' (Hutchinson)

shows: represents.

l.32.   solemnitie: solemn ceremony.

l.33.   herse: bier. In Herbert's day the word did not signify a funeral carriage.

73. DECAY

l.1.   lodge with Lot: See Gen. 19.3.

l.2.   Struggle with Jacob: See Gen. 32.24.

sit with Gideon: See Judg. 6.11.

l.3.　*Advise with Abraham:* See Gen. 18.

ll.3–5.　*when thy power . . . Let me alone:* 'Even though you told him to "let you alone", Moses was on such familiar terms with you that with his "strong complaints and mone" he could persuade you to give in.' See Exod. 32.9–14, especially 10: 'Now therefore let me alone, that my wrath may wax hot against them.'

l.7.　*At some fair oak:* i.e. where the Lord 'sat with Gideon' (Judg. 6.11).
　　bush: the burning bush where God appeared to Moses (Exod. 3.2).
　　cave: The word of the Lord came to Elijah in a cave (1 Kings 19.9).
　　well: where Abraham's servant met Rebekah (Gen. 24.11).

l.9.　See Exod. 19.20.

l.10.　See Exod. 28.33–5, and *Aaron l*.3.

l.12.　See Luke 17.21.

l.15.　*thirds:* a legal term (usually used in the plural) meaning especially 'the third of the personal property of a deceased husband allowed to his widow' (*O.E.D.*). Sin and Satan, already in possession of two thirds of the heart, plan to gain God's third.

l.16.　*when as:* seeing that, inasmuch as.

l.17.　*once spread:* once widespread.

73.　JORDAN (II)

For discussion of this poem and *Jordan* (*I*) see Introduction, p. 18.

Title: See note to *Jordan* (*I*), p. 135. In W. this poem is entitled *Invention*. It has several similarities both in thought and phrase (see notes below) with Sidney's first sonnet of *Astrophel and Stella*, where the word 'invention' occurs three times, and with his third.

l.3.　Sidney, Sonnet 1, *ll*.5–6: 'I sought fit words to paint the blackest face of woe; /Studying inventions fine.'
　　invention: See *Love I l*.6 and note.

l.4.　*burnish:* 'To grow plump, or stout, to spread out; to increase in breadth.' (*O.E.D.*)

l.5.　See *Dulnesse ll*.7–8.

l.6.　*to sell:* for sale.

l.8.　*if I were not sped:* 'If I did not meet with success.'

l.10.　*quick:* alive, or lively (in antithesis to 'dead').

l.12.　*those joyes:* i.e. heavenly joys.
　　his: its, i.e. the sun's.

l.16.　*wide:* i.e. wide of the mark.

ll.17–18. Sidney, Sonnet 1, *l*.44: 'Foole said My muse to mee, looke in thy heart and write.' Sonnet 3, *ll*.13–14: 'then all my deed/But copying is.'

74. CONSCIENCE

l.6. 'All that I hear or see is distorted.'

ll.13–24. 'The remedy ("receit") will be Christ's; when I taste it at the communion table it cleanses me so that conscience can no longer accuse. However, if conscience continues to worry me, apart from this treatment there is something which can be used directly against conscience itself: I have a bill-hook (i.e. the Cross) to use against those that trouble me. Thus the Cross both provides the blood which cleanses me, and is my sword with which I am able to fight conscience.'

ll.21–2. Psalm 23.4–5 (*B.C.P.*): 'thy rod and thy staff comfort me. Thou shalt prepare a table before me against them that trouble me.'

ll.23–4. See Donne, *The Crosse l*.25: 'Materiall Crosses then, good physicke bee.'

75. THE QUIP

As in *The Pearl* Herbert affirms his love for God in a simple statement of devotion which acts as a refrain to the four central stanzas, and in which the repartee, the smart reply, or 'quip', is left to God. Although Herbert pretends to deny himself the 'quick Wit' that properly belongs to God (*ll*.17–20) the poem is in fact packed with it—as for instance in line 19, in which, during the very process of denouncing 'quick Wit', Herbert makes a quibble or 'quip': 'And, to be short, make an Oration'. The final and most ambiguous verbal equivocation, the poem's quip *par excellence*, comes at the close, where God is granted the essence of wit and brevity: 'say, I am thine'. It is difficult not to see here a double meaning—one which serves to reinforce Herbert's involvement with God. Depending on whether 'I am thine' is a direct or an indirect statement we have the two readings, 'say, "I (God) am thine (Herbert's)" ', and 'say that I (Herbert) am thine (God's)'. The final line, 'And then they have their answer home', is thus a delightful joke on Herbert's part, for the 'answer' is the poem's most ambiguous—even though reassuringly ambiguous— statement.

Title: The above should indicate that 'quip' can mean both 'A sharp or sarcastic remark directed against a person' (*O.E.D.*), and, more particularly, 'A verbal equivocation, a quibble' (*O.E.D.*). See Shakespeare, *1 Henry IV*, I.ii.43: 'How now, how now, mad wag? What, in thy quips and thy quiddities?' and *Much Ado*, II.iii.228: 'Small quips and sentences and these paper bullets of the brain.'

l.2.   *train-bands:* abbreviated from 'trained bands', the trained companies of citizen soldiery of London.

l.7.   i.e. why do you not clutch at beauty? See *The Collar l.*18.

l.8.   Psalm 38.15 (*B.C.P.*): 'For in thee, O Lord, have I put my trust: thou shalt answer for me, O Lord my God.'

l.9.   *still:* always.

*l.*15.   This is difficult: 'He granted me only a glimpse (of Court life)', or perhaps, 'He scarcely recognized me'. Palmer suggests, 'He declared that a person of my dull life could only half perceive what glory is.'

*l.*19.   *Oration:* B. 'oration' 1633. Herbert may be mocking himself as Public Orator at Cambridge.

*l.*23.   *Speak not at large:* i.e. speak briefly, in contrast to 'make an Oration' of *l.*19. *large;* B. 'large,' 1633.

*l.*24.   *home:* an adverb; right to the heart of the matter.

76. DIALOGUE

The dialogue form was a favourite of Herbert's; see for instance in this selection *Love* (*III*). Notice the sustained legal and trading metaphors in the poem, and compare *Redemption*.

*ll.*1–8.   'If I thought my soul worth thy having, I would not hesitate to surrender it, but, since all my care spent upon it cannot give it worth (*gains*, *l.*6), how can I expect thee to benefit by acquiring it?' (Hutchinson)

l.4.   *waving:* perhaps a variant of 'waver' (see Jam. 1.6), to vacillate. But it is also an old spelling of 'waive', a legal term meaning 'to decline an offer or not assert a right'.

*l.*16.   *transferr'd:* a legal term: 'To convey or make over (title, right, property) by deed or legal process.' (*O.E.D.*)

*l.*20.   *savour:* 'Perception, understanding.' (*O.E.D.*, citing this example.)

*l.*22.   See John 14.6.

*l.*23.   *disclaim:* 'To renounce, relinquish, or repudiate a legal claim.' (*O.E.D.*)

*ll.*25–6.   'That disclaimer of yours is enough, if only you can make it without regret;' but 'repining' is meant, no doubt, to refer both to the Saviour and to Herbert.

*l.*27.   *clay,* B. 'clay' no comma 1633.

*l.*28.   'You would follow the example of my renunciation.'

.30. *desert:* the word was pronounced, and often spelt, 'desart', as in Marvell's *To his Coy Mistress.*

77. DULNESSE

For discussion see Introduction p. 18.

.2. See note to *ll.*11–15 of *Employment (II)*, p. 140.

.3. *quicknesse:* vitality of mind.

.5. *curious:* elaborately made.

.12. *Pure red and white:* a conceit on the agony and beauty of Christ taken by Herbert from the secular love poets. He is also making use of an established tradition of Christ as lover; see especially Song of Solomon 5.10: 'My beloved is white and ruddy'.

*l.*13–15. *When all perfections . . . very dust:* 'When all perfections meet in one—and that one perfection reveals only *your* form is made up of all those many perfections—then the very dust . . .'

.18. *window-songs:* serenades.

.19. *pretending:* in the old sense of 'to make a suit for' (*O.E.D.*).

.21. *sugred lyes:* see *The Rose l.*2.

78. HOPE

The symbols 'seem almost to be used in a way familiar to the mathematician; as when a set of letters may stand for any numbers of a certain sort, and you are not curious to know which numbers are meant because you are only interested in the relations between them'. (William Empson, *Seven Types of Ambiguity*, Chap. 3. The reader should look at his complete analysis of the poem.)

Before trying to sort out any significances in this poem it is essential to experience it at first hand, to feel the tensions which the symbols create. Each carries overtones of expectation and disappointment such as might be experienced in any situation of trial and endeavour. The richly suggestive nature of the symbols and the lack of reference to specific events should make the reader wary of a too narrow and definitive interpretation. The following notes are only an attempt to indicate the way in which different and apparently contradictory interpretations are possible and are all part of the poem's significance.

.1. *a watch:* a reminder to Hope of the brevity of life; or of the amount of time already spent in expectation; a hint that the time for the fulfilment of hopes is due.

l.2.   *An anchor:* power of endurance; no immediate expectation of progress in the fulfilment of his hopes; the certainty of redemption. Heb. 6.19: 'Which hope we have as an anchor of the soul, both sure and stedfast.'

l.3.   *an old prayer-book:* prayers long used in constant devotion; an ordered rule of life.

l.4.   *an optick:* either refers to a telescope—the faith that searches the heavens; an aid to perceive fulfilment which is at a great distance: or to a microscope—the necessity for a closer look at his 'old prayer-book', to examine more closely his way of life.

l.5.   *a viall full of tears:* as a mark of repentance; at the pain of unfulfilled hopes; at the pain of past renunciations.

l.6.   *green eares:* indication of present immaturity; promise that spiritual growth will come; at the same time an indication that much time will be needed for the harvest to ripen.

l.8.   *a ring:* the perfect ring of Heaven or eternity, as in Vaughan, *The World*, *ll.*1–2:

> I saw Eternity the other night
> Like a great Ring of pure and endless light.

Perhaps the 'ring' symbolizes marriage with God through the Church.

79.   SINNES ROUND

As in *Deniall* and *A Wreath* Herbert uses deliberate artifice to strengthen the thought of the poem—in this case the self-perpetuating character of sin. Donne used the same technique in his *La Corona* sonnets, where the last line of each sonnet is repeated as the first line of the next, and the last line of the final sonnet is the first line of the first.

l.4.   *cockatrice:* Sir Thomas Browne describes the cockatrice, a fabulous creature otherwise known as the basilisk, in *Pseudodoxia Epidemica*, Bk. 3, Chap. 7: 'it killeth at a distance', 'poisoneth by the eye', and 'it proceedeth from a Cock's egg hatched under a Toad or Serpent.' Isa. 59.5: the wicked 'hatch cockatrice' eggs . . . he that eateth of their eggs dieth, and that which is crushed breaketh out into a viper.'

l.8.   *the Sicilian hill:* Mount Etna.

l.9.   *vent:* 'To discharge, eject, cast or pour out' (*O.E.D.*). But the intro-duction of 'wares' gives the secondary meaning 'To sell or vend' (*O.E.D.*).

l.10.   The cockatrice was supposed to kill by its breath.

l.15.   See Gen. 11.4–8.

   dissensions: B. 'dissentions' 1633.

79. CONFESSION

l.5. *till:* not, as now, for cash, but any small box or drawer forming part of a larger box, chest, etc.

l.8. *work and winde:* see *Jordan (II) l.*13.

l.12. Herbert's *Outlandish Proverbs*, No. 475: 'Wealth is like rheume, it falles on the weakest parts.'

l.15. *foot:* 'To seize or clutch with the talons' (*O.E.D.*). This is usually used of birds of prey.

l.16. *give out:* desist.

*ll.*19–20. because there is 'no fastning' (*l.*23); 'a deliberate paradox, of the sort embedded in traditional Christian teaching, but "turned" by Herbert very much to his own uses.' (Douglas Brown, *Selected Poems of George Herbert.*)

*ll.*29–30. *let them . . . my breast:* 'At their best the brightest day and the clearest diamond will appear opaque and cloudy compared with my breast (when it is cleared by confession).'

80. GIDDINESSE

l.3. *sev'rall:* distinct and separate.

l.11. *snudge:* 'To remain snug and quiet' (*O.E.D.*, citing this example); but a different verb, meaning 'To be miserly, stingy', would tie in well with the reference to food in the previous line.

l.12. *spares:* i.e. is sparing.

*ll.*19–20. 'Not the mammal like a porpoise, but the dorado . . . popularly called a dolphin, a fish like a mackerel; its metallic colours undergo rapid changes on its being taken out of the water and about to die, but it cannot be inferred that the changes have any relation to its *desires*.' (Hutchinson)

l.27. *Except thou make us dayly:* 2 Cor. 4.16: 'though our outward man perish, yet the inward man is renewed day by day.'

82. THE BUNCH OF GRAPES

For discussion see Introduction, p. 16.

*ll.*1–2. There is possibly an ambiguity: 'I possessed, locked up within me, Christ's joy, His love, but someone has let it out, and now it escapes me;' or, 'I locked up and denied myself pleasure, the bad kind of joy, but it has been let out.'

l.4. *Sev'n yeares ago:* probably used as a round number. There is no way of telling whether the reference is autobiographical.

vogue 'General course or tendency.' (*O.E.D.*, citing this example.)

*ll.*6–7. The Israelites' rebellion when nearing Canaan, the Promised land, caused God to decree the wandering in the desert back towards the Red Sea. See Num. 14.25 and 33.10.

*ll.*10–14. See 1 Cor. 10.6 and 11.

*l.*10. *spann'd:* measured out, limited.

*l.*11. i.e. the Israelites' story is our story.

*l.*12. 'Nothing which has moved men widely is an individual affair. (Palmer)

*l.*13. *let in future times:* i.e. are true for all time.

*l.*14. 'His justice to the Jews will be the same as his justice to us for our crimes.'

*l.*15. See Num. 9.15.

*l.*16. *Our Scripture-dew:* Num. 11.9: 'And when the dew fell upon the camp in the night, the manna fell upon it.'

*l.*17. *shrowds:* 'a shelter, esp. one of a slight or temporary kind, as a tent.' (*O.E.D.*)

*l.*19. *cluster:* See Num. 13.23. It was after the 'cluster of grapes' had been brought out of Canaan to the Israelites that the people rebelled, refusing the joy which the grapes represented.

*l.*24. *Noah's vine:* See Gen. 9.20. The vineyard of Noah (of whom 'the whole earth was overspread', Gen. 9.19) was abused just as were the grapes of Eschol, and under the old Law both abuses resulted in a curse. This is in contrast to the new dispensation made by Christ on the Cross.

*l.*28. *himself,* 1633. 'himselfe' no comma B.

  pressed: See Isa. 63.3; also *The Agonie*, and notes.

John 15.1: 'I am the true vine, and my Father is the husbandman.'

83. MANS MEDLEY

Title: 'Medley' is 'A combination or mixture' and was originally used without a disparaging sense (*O.E.D.*). But the word also means 'A cloth woven with wools of different colours or shades' (*O.E.D.*), and Herbert is undoubtedly thinking of this in lines 15–18.

*ll.*7–12. 'Mere sentient creatures have a right only to life on earth, and angels only to heaven; man, however, alone possesses both joys, those of earth and heaven.' For the belief that man was the centre of the universe see introductory note to *Man* (p. 144).

*ll.*15–18. 'Man should take his rank not by the coarse material of his animal nature, but according to ("After", *l.*18) the delicately made ("curious", *l.*16) trimming of his higher spiritual nature.'

round: term used for a cloth made of thick thread.

ground: 'a piece of cloth used as a basis for embroidery or decoration. (*O.E.D.*)

*l.*27. *two winters:* i.e. one physical ('frosts') and one spiritual ('thoughts').

*l.*30. *two deaths:* the natural death of the body, and the eternal death of the soul if condemned at the Last Judgment. See Rev. 20.6 and 14, and Rev. 21.8.

84. DIVINITIE

*l.*2. *spheres:* refers to the old astronomers' concept of concentric hollow globes revolving round the earth (see note to *l.*2 of *Vanitie* (*I*)).

*l.*3. *clod:* a clodhopper, a blockhead; perhaps a ploughman.

*l.*8. *lies by:* remains unexercised.

*l.*9. The metaphor of Christ at the Crucifixion being a barrel of wine pierced for man's sake is used in the last stanza of *The Agonie* (see note to *ll.*14-15, p. 127).

*ll.*11-12. John 19.23-4: 'Then the soldiers, when they had crucified Jesus, took . . . his coat: now the coat was without seam, woven from the top throughout. They said therefore among themselves, Let us not rend it, but cast lots for it, whose it shall be.' God's wisdom, like the coat after the Crucifixion, is not slashed ('jagg'd') into pieces, into 'questions and divisions' but, like the coat, remains a unity.

*l.*15. *which only save:* 'are the only ones which save.'

*ll.*21-4. The Gordian knot of transubstantiation, of wine into blood, is expressed by Herbert in an inverted form, as Coleridge (notes to *The Temple*) points out: 'Nay the contrary; take wine to be blood, and *the* blood of a man who died 1800 years ago.' See also *ll.*17-18 of *The Agonie*, and note. The point of this stanza is that God's love must be tasted rather than defined.

*l.*25. *Epicycles:* 'A small circle, having its centre on the circumference of a greater circle . . . In the Ptolemaic system of astronomy each of the "seven planets" was supposed to revolve in an epicycle, the centre of which moved along a greater circle.' (*O.E.D.*)

*l.*27. *staffe:* See *The Agonie*, *l.*3 and note.

'The allegorical form is of course a reminder that what we are concerned with is a graph of more than one kind of experience, but at no point in the poem are we simply interpreting an allegory; the bitter poignancy of the conclusion springs from deeply personal feelings that we have been made to share.' (L. C. Knights, 'George Herbert', essay in *Explorations*.)

l.7.   *Fancies:* B. 'phansies' 1633.

l.10.   i.e. life was passing.

l.11.   *Cares:* B. 'cares' 1633.

l.13.   *Passion:* B. 'passion' 1633.

l.14.   *wold:* may be a pun on 'would' (the reading of B.).

l.17.   *Angell:* a gold coin with the device of the archangel Michael on it. Donne uses at length the same pun in his elegy *The Bracelet*. Herbert is thinking of his guardian angel; and also perhaps of his marriage to Jane Danvers, the 'friend' being Henry Danvers.

l.36.   *a chair:* as a place of comfort; probably also the sedan-chair, as a means of travel. See also note to *l.29* of *Mortification*, p. 147.

86. THE HOLDFAST

A sonnet in the Shakespearean pattern. The paradoxes of Christian faith are here given poetic expression. Herbert's mentor speaks, or is reported as speaking, in lines 3–4, 6–7, 9–10; 'a friend' speaks in line 12, and possibly in lines 13–14.

Title: probably from Psalm 73.27 (*B.C.P.*): 'But it is good for me to hold me fast by God.'

l.6.   *was:* indicates that the next line is a direct quotation.

l.13.   See 1 Cor. 15.22.

87. PRAISE (II)

This poem is in imitation of Psalm 116.

l.4.   *move:* press, urge, prompt; affect with emotion.

l.14.   *cleare:* acquit.

ll.15–16.   The placing of 'alone' suggests both, 'You had ears only for me, despite the noisy reply of my sins' and, 'You are the only one who listened to me when my sins still clamoured against me.'

ll.19–20.   God is 'never so high but it lies within the heart's real capacity to set Him higher ("I *can* raise thee"). Then the qualifying clause "though not in heaven" enriches the meaning further. He is unimaginably beyond any adequate praising by any human heart, "high as the heavens are from the earth" . . . The heart that raises up its Lord is conscious how far from being itself "in heaven" it is, by the very need of so exerting itself to raise Him.' (Douglas Brown, *Selected Poems of George Herbert*.)

*ll.*21–4.   The hymn-books omit this stanza.

*l.*26.   *enroll:* 'to record with honour, celebrate.' (*O.E.D.*)

*l.*28.   *extoll:* 'To lift up, raise' (*O.E.D.*), and 'to praise highly.' (*O.E.D.*)

88.   THE COLLAR

For discussion see Introduction, p. 29.

Title: 'Collar' is a symbol of discipline, and the word was often used figuratively in expressions like 'to slip the collar'. Herbert wants to slip his neck from the collar of God's service. The title does not refer to the modern clerical collar.

*l.*1.   *board:* table; God's board, communion table.

*l.*5.   *store:* abundance.

*l.*6.   'Shall I always be doing service to another?'

*l.*14.   *bayes:* laurel crown.

*l.*16.   *wasted:* laid waste.

*l.*21.   *not. Forsake:* B. 'not forsake' 1633.

*l.*29.   *Call in thy deaths head:* take away the skull, i.e. *memento mori.*

*l.*35.   *Child!* B. 'Childe:' 1633.

89.   THE GLIMPSE

*ll.*8–10.   'At least if you were more like waves and wind your appearances and reappearances would cause less permanent damage; or (even better) if you were like flowers your appearance would be more lasting.'

*ll.*13–15.   'Lime asked for water to cool its heat, but the addition of water only increased it.' Thus delight, which should refresh like water, only makes the poet burn the more. The phrase 'of old (they say)' suggests that Herbert is alluding to some fable or allegory.

*l.*18.   *his:* its, i.e. the heart's.

*l.*19.   'While my fears foretold the probable brevity of delight's stay, the heart replies to the fears . . .' The reply of the heart is given in the next line.

*l.*20.   *Outlandish Proverbs,* No. 726: 'A gentle heart is tyed with an easie thread.'

*ll.*23–5.   'Although your store of heavenly delights is rightly locked away for future use, occasional "droppings" from it (like the crumbs of *l*.17) may come to me without the main supply being touched.'

*ll.*26–7. *stay* may mean 'staying here', in which case the interpretation would be, 'While you are here I shall keep my wheel going, making indeed your stay seem short.' It is more probable, however, that 'stay' means 'staying away, absence', in which case we have Hutchinson's alternative interpretations: 'I will spin so busily that the time of thy staying away will seem short; or, I will contentedly keep the wheel going, and not let grief and sin interrupt my work, provided (*so that l*.27) thy absence does not last too long.'

*ll.*29–30. The antecedent of 'Who' is 'me'.

91. CLASPING OF HANDS

See Introduction, p. 13.

l.1. See Song of Solomon 2.16.

l.3. *Then:* than

  or . . . or: either . . . or.

l.6. *advantage:* addition.

  more no punctuation: B. 'more.' 1633.

*ll.*12–13. *something more . . . then thine:* 'I may take the liberty of calling you to some extent more mine than your own.'

91. JOSEPHS COAT

Joseph's 'coat of many colours', which here represents the mixture of joys and sorrows in the Christian life, is a sign of his father's love (Gen. 37.3); because a single grief, if run to its conclusion, would overthrow the poet, relief is afforded in his ability to make music of his sorrows. Thus life, like the coat, is variegated.

Rosemond Tuve (*A Reading of George Herbert* pp. 175–80) gives a most stimulating interpretation based on a traditional parallel of Joseph with Christ, of Joseph's coat with Christ's flesh at the Crucifixion: 'the title serves to indicate a common Christian idea, "Take up thy Cross . . ."— i.e. the eternal repetition, in men, of Christ's struggle, in the coat of his flesh, with the anguish which is the other side of all human joy'.

l.6. *his:* its.

l.8. *both:* i.e. both 'grief and smart' and the 'heart'.

l.9. *both:* here seems to refer to the 'heart' and the 'bodie'.

  being due to: i.e. belonging to.

l.10. *he hath spoil'd the race:* by preventing grief and the heart killing the body (see 'runne' *l*.8). Tuve compares this phrase with *The Reprisall*, where God has outgone the poet in griefs through the sufferings of the Passion.
l.11. *ticing:* i.e. enticing.

92. THE PULLEY

This poem recalls the story of Pandora, the first mortal woman. Jupiter gave her a box containing all the blessings of the gods, which, on its being opened, escaped and were lost, except for hope, which was at the bottom of the box.

Title: Though the word 'pulley' is not used in the poem the implication of the conclusion is that weariness will hoist or 'tosse' man up to God as with a pulley.

l.5. *span:* 'a very small extent or space.' (*O.E.D.*, citing this example.)

l.10. *Rest:* The play upon this word runs through the following stanzas (see *ll*.14, 16, 17). As well as the more familiar meanings (repose, *l*.10; remainder, *l*.16) the mention of wealth and gains ('treasure', *l*.9; 'jewell', *l*.12; 'rich', *l*.18) indicates a reference to the card game primero, where 'rest' is 'the stakes kept in reserve . . . and upon the loss of which the game is terminated' (*O.E.D.*)

l.15. *both:* i.e. God and man.

93. THE PRIESTHOOD

See introductory note to *The Windows*, p. 138. Notice the varying significance of the image of the potter's clay throughout this poem. God compared to a potter working on his clay is a familiar Biblical image; Isa. 64.8: 'we are the clay, and thou our potter.' See also Jer. 18.6 and Rom. 9.21–3.

ll.5–6. *exchanging . . . holy word:* Isa. 49.2: 'And he hath made my mouth like a sharp sword.' 'The third day after he was made Rector of Bemerton, and had changed his sword and silk clothes into a canonical hat. . . .' (Walton, *Lives*).

l.10. *compositions:* 'Mental constitution, or constitution of mind and body combined.' (*O.E.D.*)

l.16. *That earth is fitted by the fire:* See *l*.8, 'I but earth and clay', and *l*.7, 'thou art fire'.

l.25. For instance God called St. Paul 'a chosen vessel unto me, to bear my name before the Gentiles, and kings, and the children of Israel'. (Acts 9.15.)

*l.*28.   *convey:* B. 'conuey' 1633.

*ll.*31–3.   2 Sam. 6.6: 'Uzzah put forth his hand to the ark of God, and took hold of it; for the oxen shook it.' As a consequence he was struck dead by God.

*ll.*39–42.   'The modest by observing a respectful deference pay a better homage than the proud who seek to keep up their state by a rival magnificence. Herbert may hope to commend himself for the priesthood by his humility.' (Hutchinson)

94.   GRIEF

*l.*2.   See Jer. 9.1.

*l.*10.   *a lesse world:* man, the microcosm. See *Man*, and introductory note. Even the 'greater' world, the macrocosm, is 'but small' to Herbert.

*l.*11.   *A narrow cupboard:* See *Man l.*29.

*l.*15.   *feet:* a pun on metrical feet and the running of tears.

95.   THE CROSSE

Although undoubtedly written some years after *Affliction* (*I*), when Herbert was priest at Bemerton, *The Crosse* is also a poem of deep internal conflict. His anxiety is no longer over choice of vocation, but an incapacity through ill health to answer the demands of that vocation. As in *Affliction* (*I*) mere hints in the language indicate the poet's real shortcomings; notice in the first three stanzas the frequent reference to 'I', 'my', 'me', betraying an excessive self-awareness (compare *Affliction* (*I*), 'yet me from my wayes taking', *l.*54), and the pride of lines 5–6.

Title: 'The title seems to have double force; both that made explicit in the last stanza turning upon the desire sufficiently to serve and to do honour to Christ who suffered; and that implicit in the notion that each has his cross to bear.' (Douglas Brown, *Selected Poems of George Herbert.*)

*l.*5.   *wealth* no comma: B. 'wealth,' 1633.

*l.*8.   *this deare end:* i.e. the priesthood.

*l.*12.   *threatnings:* As Louis L. Martz (*The Poetry of Meditation*) points out, 'clearly not used with the normal implications, but appears to mean something like "offerings".' He suggests that the usage is related to the old verb 'threap', to offer positively.

*l.*16.   *harmonie*): Colon added by Hutchinson.

*l.*18.   'except when I contemplate the cross, whose strength forces me into action.'

l.19.   *sort:* come about, turn out.

l.22.   See Psalm 102.10 (*B.C.P.*).

l.23.   *sped:* accomplished successfully.

l.29.   *delicates:* luxuries.

l.30.   *a weed:* i.e. useless, as in *Employment (I) l*.22.

l.36.   *my words:* i.e. your words which I now make mine.

96. THE FLOWER

For discussion see Introduction p. 23.

In *The Temple* (as in this selection) *The Flower* follows, and counter-balances, *The Crosse*, where Herbert laments the 'contarieties' which he is here celebrating. Coleridge (note to *The Temple*) called this 'a delicious poem'.

ll.2–4.   *ev'n as . . . pleasure bring: demean* means 'bearing', as in 'demeanour' (*O.E.D.*), and can also be a form of 'demesne', estate or condition (*O.E.D.*). The general sense, however, is little affected: 'the spring flowers not only have their own intrinsic beauty, but they are also welcome as a sign of the passing of winter.' (Hutchinson)

l.16.   *quickning:* restoring life.

l.18.   Bells which are chimed (i.e. swung just enough to make the clappers strike) produce a musical and varied sound, whereas a 'passing bell' is tolled at the hour of death, slowly and on a single note.

ll.19–20.   'We are wrong to say a thing exists of itself, unchangeably.'

l.21.   *spell:* interpret.

l.25.   *Offring at:* aiming at.

l.28.   *joining:* i.e. to produce tears.

ll.32–5.   'Is there any frost as cold as your anger? Compared with your slightest frown even the Arctic and Antarctic poles seem like torrid zones.'

l.44.   *glide:* slip gently and imperceptibly away.

l.45.   *Which:* i.e. this knowledge.

98. DOTAGE

l.1.   *glozing:* flatteringly deceptive. Milton, *Paradise Lost*, III.93: 'For Man will heark'n to his glozing lies.'

   casks: barrels. 'The word *cask* was sometimes used for *casket . . .* and may here suggest valuable cases with nothing of worth inside them.' (Hutchinson)

l.2.   *Foolish night-fires:* 'An ignis fatuus, will o' the wisp.' (*O.E.D.*, citing this example only.)

l.3. *Chases in Arras:* hunting scenes depicted on tapestries, as opposed to the 'Sure-footed griefs' of *l*.9.

l.4. *in a career:* i.e. in full tilt.

l.5. *nothing between two dishes:* a Spanish proverb: 'Nada entre duos platos.'

l.8. *in grain:* phrase short for 'dyed in grain'. Often, as here, used figuratively: 'indelible, ineradicable' (*O.E.D.*). Herbert may be punning on the 'grain' of corn: 'anguish that is fully ripening', just as the 'vexations' are 'ripe and blown'.

99. THE SONNE

l.3. *coast:* region, country.

l.8. *Chasing:* chasing away, dispelling. When the father's light of life grows dim the son takes it up.

l.14. The pun was common in Herbert's day. See for instance Donne, *La Corona* 7, *l*.2: 'Joy at the uprising of this Sunne, and Sonne.'

99. A TRUE HYMNE

The reader would do well to compare the thought and technique of this poem with others containing brief refrains which, like 'My joy, my life, my crown', run 'mutt'ring up and down' in Herbert's verse; thus *Antiphon* (*I*) ('My God and King'), *The Quip* ('But thou shalt answer, Lord, for me'), *The Forerunners* ('Thou art still my God'), *The Posie* ('Lesse then the least of all thy mercies').

l.9. *finenesse:* subtlety, or splendour; perhaps both.

l.14. *somewhat is behinde:* something is lacking.

l.15. *in kinde:* according to the true nature of a hymn.

100. THE ANSWER

l.3. *bandie:* 'To throw or strike (a ball) to and fro as in the games of tennis and bandy.' (*O.E.D.*)

ll.4–5. *like summer . . . sunne-shine:* 'friends who swarm like summer flies about one who is prosperous, and while the sun shines on them;' but who drop away in times of adversity.

l.8. *exhalation:* a mist, vapour.

l.9. *means:* aims at.

l.10. *pursie:* swollen, heavy.

ll.13–14. Whatever 'the answer' to this poem, there is no doubt that

Herbert wanted deliberately to tease his readers. Perhaps he intended to leave the poem as an example of riddling wit, with the implication 'the answer is that there is no answer'; perhaps he wished us to supply some such reply as 'Lord, have mercy upon me'; or the implication may be 'God indeed knows what the answer is, but I don't'. Joan Bennett (Review of Hutchinson's ed. in *Review of English Studies*, Vol. 17, 1941) ingeniously suggests that 'the rest' may mean not only 'the rest of Herbert's life story summarized in the poem', but also 'the freedom from toil or care associated with the future life' (*O.E.D.* 4b). She concludes: 'the angels and blessed spirits know, even better than he himself does, whether or not he could reply to his critics, "I am God's servant despite all my losses and failures".'

101. THE 23D PSALME

In his rendering of this psalm Herbert makes use of both the A.V., and the Coverdale version in the *B.C.P.* He must also have been familiar with the versions in Sternhold and Hopkins' *Metrical Versions of the Psalms*.

l.2.   There are two versions of the psalm in Sternhold and Hopkins. The first contains this line.

l.3.   Song of Solomon 2.16: 'My beloved is mine, and I am his.' See also *Clasping of Hands l.1.*

l.9.   *convert:* Though the religious sense is also implied, *O.E.D.*, citing this example, defines: 'To turn back, cause to return.'

l.10.   *in frame:* into a suitable disposition. The second version in Sternhold and Hopkins contains this line.

l.16.   *thy staffe to bear:* ' "to bear me up", provide me with support. There may be some suggestion of "giving me my bearings".' (Douglas Brown, *Selected Poems of George Herbert*.)

l.22.   *measure:* 'To be commensurate with.' (*O.E.D.*, citing this example.)

102. AARON

See Exodus 28. To carry out his priestly function and bring peace to his people Aaron had to wear the divinely prescribed garments. Grierson's notion, followed by most commentators, that 'each verse . . . suggests metrically the swelling and dying sound of a bell; and, like a bell, the rhymes reiterate the same sound' is highly improbable. The purpose of the repeated rhyme-words is to represent the unchanging ideals symbolized by Aaron's ceremonial garments. The outward garments, the ideals, do not change, but the inward man, in order to attain those ideals, must become complete by joining with Christ. Only then is Herbert ready to perform his priestly function.

l.1.   A gold plate on Aaron's mitre was to be engraved with the words 'Holiness to the Lord' (Exod. 28.36).

l.2.   Into his breastplate (or pouch) Aaron was instructed to put the oracular stones Urim and Thummin—the Hebrew for 'lights' and 'perfections' (Exod. 28.30).

ll.3–4.   About the hem of Aaron's robe were bells and pomegranates (Exod. 28.33–5). Bells had become a traditional symbol for the preacher's voice proclaiming the Gospel.

l.8.   *noise of passions:* i.e. a clamour, as opposed to the 'Harmonious bells' of *l.*3 and 'Another musick' of *l.*13.

l.18.   *striking me ev'n dead:* 'striking' is a pun—'striking me dead', and 'ringing me (as the clapper strikes the bell) even though I am dead'.

ll.19–20.   'So that I may rest to the old Adam, and be regenerated in Christ.' See Col. 3.9–10.

l.24.   *But lives in me:* This and the thought of the last two stanzas relate to Gal. 2.20: 'I am crucified with Christ: nevertheless I live; yet not I, but Christ liveth in me.'

103.   THE FORERUNNERS

l.1.   *harbingers:* messengers sent in advance of a royal progress to secure lodgings by chalking the doors—hence the 'mark' here, and *l.*35.

l.2.   The whiteness of the poet's hair is the mark of death's harbinger. Herbert goes on to ask, must his mental powers also be threatened?

l.3.   *dispark*= disimpark (*O.E.D.*, citing this example), to turn out of a park. Must the 'sparkling notions' be turned out of his brain?

l.6.   *Thou art still my God:* Psalm 31.16 (*B.C.P.*): 'But my hope hath been in thee, O Lord: I have said, Thou art my God.'

ll.9–10.   'I do not care what becomes of the rest, so long as the "Thou art still my God" is in no danger of being taken from me.'

l.11.   *dittie:* 'The words of a song, as distinguished from the music or tune; also, the leading theme or phrase; hence, Subject, matter, theme, "burden".' (*O.E.D.*)

l.19.   *Lovely:* 1633 second ed. 'Louely' B. and 1633 first ed.

l.26.   *canvas:* coarse cloth, still used for clothing at this time.

l.31.   *I passe not:* again, 'I care not'.

l.33.   *say.* B. 'say,' 1633.

104. THE ROSE

l.6. *Colour'd:* i.e. disguised, made to seem what they are not; also a literal reference, as 'Blushing' in the next line indicates.

ll.9–10. Herbert as it were slips up, continuing to call 'delights' deceptions.

l.14. *what you now advise:* i.e. 'to take more pleasure' (*l*.1).

l.18. *it purgeth:* See *Life l*.15, and note. In Herbert's poem *Providence* is the line, 'A rose, besides his beautie, is a cure'.

ll.19–20. *forbearance:* abstinence. 'Its purging quality discloses the rose to be our enemy, and we should therefore avoid it;' just as pleasure produces repentance, which is likewise a purge (*ll*.27–8).

l.24. The rose, like worldly pleasures, is painful in its death ('close').

l.31. *fairly:* 'It is fair, just, that I should so oppose you;' and, 'I oppose you with a beautiful example,' i.e. without bitterness, gracefully.

105. THE POSIE

At the end of his preface to *The Temple* Nicholas Ferrar wrote: 'We conclude all with his own Motto, with which he used to conclude all things that might seem to tend any way to his own honour; *Lesse then the least of Gods mercies*.' See also the words Walton reported Herbert as saying on entrusting his 'little Book' to Ferrar, Introduction p. 11.

Title: The meaning of 'posy' here is 'a short motto, originally a line or verse of poetry . . . inscribed within a ring, etc.' (*O.E.D.*). Herbert uses the word elsewhere with this and other meanings; see *The Thanksgiving l*.14, and note, *Life l*.1, and note.

ll.3–4. In Gen. 32.10 Jacob says: 'I am not worthy of the least of all the mercies, and of all the truth, which thou hast shewed unto thy servant.' In Eph. 3.8 St. Paul calls himself 'less than the least of all saints'.

l.9. *Invention:* See *Love I l*.6 and note; also *Jordan (II) l*.3.

106. THE ELIXIR

For discussion see Introduction p. 29.

Title: 'Elixir' is here identified with the philosopher's stone, by which the alchemists sought to transmute metals into gold; 'elixir' was also 'an essence with the property of indefinitely prolonging life' (*O.E.D.*); 'the quintessence or soul of things' (*O.E.D.*). 'In the world of particular objects, whether material or mental, the alchemists . . . seek an ultimate unity.' (Palmer)

l.7. 'always to give you a prior claim.'

l.8.   *his:* its.

l.14.   'Nothing is little in Gods service: If it once have the honour of that Name, it grows great instantly.' (*The Country Parson*, Chap. 14.)

l.15.   *his:* its.

   tincture: In alchemy this is 'a supposed spiritual principle or immaterial substance whose character or quality may be infused into material things . . .; the quintessence, spirit, or soul of a thing' (*O.E.D.*). The 'tincture' of a thing here is that it is 'for thy sake'.

l.17.   *this clause:* i.e. 'for thy sake'.

l.23.   *touch:* The word could mean, 'to test the fineness of gold . . . by rubbing it upon a touchstone' (*O.E.D.*), and also, 'to mark metal as of standard purity, etc., with an official stamp, after it had been tested' (*O.E.D.*).

107.   A WREATH

   This poem, proceeding by line-by-line repetitions and finishing at the point where it began, is itself 'A wreathed garland'. Sidney used the same method in the first lines of his Sonnet 44. Another example of circular technique in Herbert is *Sinnes Round*.

l.10.   *thy wayes* is object of both 'like' and 'know'.

107.   LOVE (III)

   This, the last poem in *The Temple*, with its delicate tone and sense of achieved serenity is perhaps one of the most perfect of English religious lyrics.

l.18.   The final 'communion' is referred to in Luke 12.37: 'Blessed are those servants, whom the lord when he cometh shall find watching; verily I say unto you, that he shall gird himself, and make them sit down to meat, and will come forth and serve them.' The difference between the situation here and in the poem is that Herbert is not 'watching'.

108.   SONNETS FROM WALTON'S 'LIVES'

   See Introduction p. 3, and introductory note to *Love* I and II, p. 132.

l.21.   *thy abuse:* an injury done to you.

l.24.   *fire:* i.e. the 'fire' of *l*.12.

l.28.   *discovery:* in the old sense of uncovering or disclosure.

INDEX OF TITLES AND FIRST LINES
OF POEMS